LANGUAGE
MADE PLAIN

by
ANTHONY BURGESS

THOMAS Y. CROWELL COMPANY
New York   •   Established 1834

To

PETER GREEN

————————————

First published in the United States of America 1965

Copyright © 1964 by Anthony Burgess

Printed in the United States of America

L. C. Card No. 65-12491

Apollo Edition, 1969

PREFACE

THIS is an introduction to the study of language and of languages. It is intended for anyone who is interested in finding out something of the mechanics and psychology of the most basic of all social functions, but my own (sometimes warring) twin vocations led me to conceive of two special kinds of audience. I am a professional novelist and critic—by which I mean that I make my living by writing works of fiction and writing about works of fiction—and so my trade is with words. I have a feeling that many other people whose trade is with words are not sufficiently concerned with finding out what words are. They are happy to join words together but not, in my view, interested in analysing their sounds, forms, and meanings. I want to try to stimulate an interest in the basic elements of which literature is made.

I address myself also, as a former teacher (both in England and abroad), to teachers of languages who feel that every pupil, in whatever kind of post-primary school, should have some basic awareness of the total linguistic process and not just a knowledge of particular languages. Indeed, I feel that no student can ever gain an intelligent knowledge of his own language, or of an imposed or elected foreign one, without knowing something of the way in which language in general works. I believe that many teachers agree with me. The second part of this book attempts to relate the learning of particular languages to the general linguistic theory that is outlined in the first part.

In many ways, this book is a primer for amateurs by an amateur. It does not dig deep, and it is far from scholarly. But it does contain the essentials, the irreducible minimum of information about language which any person who writes, reads, listens to the radio, or watches television needs to possess. We are told nowadays that, whatever our specialisation, we cannot regard ourselves as literate unless we know something of atomic physics, power politics, jurisprudence, communications, and public economics and finance. But before all these comes society, and before society comes language.

This book attempts to be objective, sceptical, scientific even, but a certain social bias is implied. The world is shrinking, supra-national communities are being painfully forged, we are all travelling more. We need to know the most efficient ways of learning other people's languages. In another sphere, we are being set upon by the most deadly propaganda machines the world has ever known, made to submit to all kinds of linguistic pressures. Let us at least try to understand what is going on. If this little work stimulates even a minimal interest in language it will not have been written in vain.

A. B.

CONTENTS

PART ONE

LANGUAGE IN GENERAL

ONE

SIGNALS IN THE DARK

1

WORDS (their meaning, spelling, pronunciation); the way foreigners talk (foreigners being everybody except us)—these frequently arouse strong feelings but very rarely much curiosity. Language tends to generate heat rather than a desire for light; the very word can be an accusation (Mr Waldo, in Dylan Thomas's *Under Milk Wood*, is guilty of, among other crimes, ' using language.') The correspondence columns of daily newspapers carry periodic wrangles about niceties of English usage, often ill-informed, sometimes fatuous. The country was once divided over the plural of ' mongoose '. I have seen grown men fighting with broken bottles (VJ Day in Gibraltar) over whether ' donkey ' meant the same thing as ' ass '. I know a family that split up for fifteen years—not a word, not a letter, not a visit—after a quarrel over the correct verbal rendering of 2s 6d. Some said it was ' two and six-pence ', others that it was ' half a crown '. One man who said it could be both was shunned by both factions. For the rest, neither side would give way; neither side would even accept the legend on the coin. In quarrels about words, people seem unwilling to see reason. Mercury, the rogue-god who presides over language, renders them blind to dictionaries and to experts. There is a general conviction that language is not a matter for experts. We all know all about language because we all use language. No similar conclusion is drawn from the fact that we all use kidneys, nerves, and intestines.

A language is a system of communication used within a particular social group. Inevitably, the emotions created by group loyalty get in the way of objective judgements about language. When we think we are making such a judgement, we are often merely making a statement about our prejudices. It is highly instructive to examine these occasionally. I myself have very powerful prejudices about what I call Americanisms. I see red whenever I read a certain popular woman columnist in a certain popular daily paper. I wait with a kind of

3

fascinated horror for her to use the locution ' I guess ', as in ' I guess he really loves you after all ' or ' I guess you'd better get yourself a new boy-friend '. I see in this form the essence of Americanism, a threat to the British Way of Life. But this is obviously nonsense, and I know it. I know that ' I guess ' is at least as old as Chaucer, pure British English, something sent over in the *Mayflower*. But, like most of us, I do not really like submitting to reason ; I much prefer blind prejudice. And so I stoutly condemn ' I guess ' as an American importation and its use by a British writer as a betrayal of the traditions of my national group.

Such condemnation can seem virtuous, because patriotism—which means loyalty to the national group—is a noble word. While virtue burns in the mind, adrenalin courses round the body and makes us feel good. Reason never has this exhilarating chemical effect. And so patriotic euphoria justifies our contempt of foreign languages and makes us unwilling to learn them properly. Chinese is still regarded in the West as a huge joke—despite what T. S. Eliot calls its ' great intellectual dignity '—and radio comedians can even raise a snigger by speaking mock-Chinese of the ' Hoo Flung Dung ' variety. Russian is, of course, nothing more than a deep vodka-rich rumble bristling with ' vitch ' and ' ski '. As for German—that is an ugly language, aggressively guttural. We rarely admit that it seems ugly because of two painful wars, that it is all a matter of association. Sometimes our automatic sneers at foreign languages are mitigated by pleasant memories—warm holidays abroad, trips to the opera. Italian can then seem beautiful, full of blue skies, *vino*, sexy tenors. Trippers to Paris, on the other hand, furtively visiting the *Folies Bergère*, project their own guilt on to the French language and see it as ' naughty ', even ' immoral '. Oo la la.

Within the national group, our prejudices tend to be very mixed and, because they operate mainly on an unconscious level, not easily recognisable. We can be natives of great cities and still find a town dialect less pleasant than a country one. And yet, hearing prettiness and quaintness in a Dorset or Devon twang, we can also despise it, because we associate it with rural stupidity or backwardness. The ugly tones of Manchester or Birmingham will, because of their great civic associations, be at the same time somehow admirable. The whole business of ugliness and beauty works strangely. A BBC announcer says ' pay day ' ; a Cockney says ' pie die '. The former is thought to be beautiful, the latter ugly, and yet the announcer can use the Cockney sounds in a statement like ' Eat that pie and you die ' without anybody's face turning sour. In fact, terms like ' ugly ' and ' beautiful ' cannot really apply to languages at all. Poets can make beautiful patterns out of words, but there are no standards we can use to formulate aesthetic judgements on the words themselves. We all have our pet hates and loves among words, but these always have to be referred to associations. A person who dislikes beetroot as a vegetable is not likely to love ' beetroot ' as a word. A poet who, in childhood, had a panful of hot stewed prunes spilled on him is, if he is a rather stupid poet, quite capable of writing ' And death, terrible as prunes '. We have to watch associations carefully, remembering that language is a public, not a private, medium, and that questions of word-hatred and word-love had best be tackled very coldly and rationally.

We are normally quick to observe regional variations in the use of the national language, but we feel less strongly about these than we do about class divisions in speech. If we speak with a Lancashire accent,* we will often be good-humoured and only slightly derisive when we hear the accent of Wolverhampton or Tyneside. Sometimes we will even express a strong admiration of alien forms of English—the speech of the Scottish Highlands, for instance, or Canadian as opposed to American. But we feel very differently about English speech when it seems to be a badge or banner of class. The dialect known variously as the Queen's English or BBC English or Standard English was, originally, a pure regional form—so-called East Midland English, with no claim to any special intrinsic merit. But it was spoken in an area that was, and still is, socially and economically pre-eminent—the area which contains London, Oxford, and Cambridge. Thus it gained a special glamour as the language of the Court and the language of learning. It has ever since—often falsely—been associated with wealth, position, and education—the supra-regional dialect of the masters, while the regional dialects remain the property of the men. In certain industrial areas it can still excite resentment, despite the fact that it no longer necessarily goes along with power or privilege. Out-of-work actors can speak it, so can underpaid schoolmasters ; tycoons, proud of their rise

* An *accent* is a set of sounds peculiar to a region, as opposed to a *dialect*, which covers, in addition to peculiarities of sound, peculiarities of grammar and vocabulary.

to the top from humble origins, will often cling to their under-privileged mother-dialect, or a slight modification of it. It is difficult for many inhabitants of a class-ridden country like ours to see virtue in Standard English or even to accept that it is possible to learn it, as one learns any foreign language. Its virtue lies in its neutrality, its lack of purely local associations, its transparency, its suitability for intellectual discourses or dispassionate Government pronouncements. It is cold, tending to wit rather than humour, the airy as opposed to the earthy.

There is room for regional dialects and room for the Queen's English. The place for the regional dialect is the region in which it was born ; it is right for the public bar, the football field, the village hop. Queen's English is for the BBC talk on Existentialism, the cocktail party, the interview for a better job. What is dangerous is the tendency among ' natural ' speakers of the Queen's English (those brought up on it from the cradle) to despise those who cannot or will not speak it themselves. The reason for this contempt is clear. The man or woman who is limited to regional speech appears to lack experience of the great world— smart restaurants, art galleries, concerts, polite talk. We are always ready to look down on people : it is an abiding pleasure, a poultice for our own sore sense of inferiority. We must think of the supra-regional advantages of the Queen's English—its universal intelligibility, its neutrality—rather than its class associations.

Snobbishness as regards speech appears when least expected, often disguised as something quite different. To return to my popular daily newspaper (which I read with the same painful pleasure as I find in the probing of a bad tooth)—this consistently uses the term ' mum ' in its articles and news-items ; not ' mum ' meaning ' silent ' but ' mum ' meaning ' mother '. I dislike the word intensely, though reason tells me that, as it is a short word, it is useful for headlines (compare ' wed ' for ' marry ' and ' bid ' for ' attempt '). Also, it is a term full of warm human connotations, highly suitable for a journal that prides itself on its warm human appeal. Yet I experience considerable revulsion when I read the following : ' PRINCESS MARGARET TO BE A MUM ' or ' MUM SEES BABY DROWN '. I try to justify this feeling by saying that ' mother ' is full of associations of great dignity, while ' mum ' is limited and vulgar. Yet I doubt if this explanation is really valid. The revulsion is too violent. I suspect the great demon of snobbishness ; a diabolic voice whispers : ' This is a working-class word. It reeks of the clothes-horse in the kitchen, bread-and-dripping by the fire. Despise it.'

Before we can study language scientifically we must strangle our group prejudices ; we must explode a great number of hoary fallacies, themselves derived from emotional attitudes. As no language is either beautiful or ugly, so no language is intrinsically either superior or inferior to another. The fact that English has become a world auxiliary is no evidence that it is a *better* language that Basque or Finnish ; its spread is the result of an historical accident which is based on a fact of geography. Languages are developed in social groups, and each group develops the language it needs. If certain primitive jungle folk have no word for ' snow ' and cannot count beyond two (sometimes we can't ourselves : *uni*lateral, *bi*lateral, *multi*lateral), they are not in the least inconvenienced : they have what they want ; when they want more they will get it. And, while it is perhaps just to hold a concept of ' primitive communities ', it is probably dangerous to talk about ' primitive languages '. In point of richness of grammar and luxuriance of vocabulary, the languages of certain ' backward ' peoples like the Eskimos are highly sophisticated.

No man, however learned or powerful, can exert control over a language, despite the ' Newspeak ' of George Orwell's *Nineteen Eighty-Four*. Languages change, and we cannot stop them from changing nor, once we are reconciled to their changing, can we determine the modes in which they shall change. It is not even possible to legislate for a language, to say what is right and what is wrong. If it is wrong to say ' you was ', then the educated men of the eighteenth century were wrong. If sluts drop their aitches, then Queen Elizabeth I was a slut. What we regard as errors are often merely survivals from an earlier form of the language. And so with seemingly eccentric usages. Characters in William Faulkner's novels of the American South say ' hit ' for ' it ' ; Lancashire dialect speakers say ' it ' for ' its ' (so did Shakespeare : ' Come to it grandam and it grandam shall give it a plum.') These are good Anglo-Saxon. They may not be in use in Standard English, but it is hard to see how they can be ' wrong '.

And so we must avoid making quick judgements, laying down the law, nursing prejudices, sneering, waving jingoistic flags, bringing a spirit of petty parochialism to the great world of human language. Languages are made by the people for the people, and people must use

language as their needs dictate. No academy has the monopoly of
' correctness ' ; no dictator knows best. If we want to understand the
phenomenon of language—and it is an astonishing one—we must
approach it in humility, letting what-should-be wait upon what-is.

Our ignorance about the fundamentals of language is not solely
derived from wilful prejudice, natural inertia, or national apathy.
Most of our school teaching of language is amateurish and incompetent :
many a sixth-form boy can read Racine with ease but have difficulty
in asking a gendarme the way to the Metro. Foreign tongues are
taught after a fashion, but language itself—its nature, function,
psychology, physiology, history—totally neglected. Our English
grammar books are shamefully out-of-date : inaccuracies of definition
and ineptitudes of terminology are perpetuated ; pointless exercises
are set ; nobody seems to care to look for the true facts of English
structure. Our teaching of foreign pronunciation is a farce. More than
all this, the tyranny of the printed or written word prevails. We still
tend to think that language is more significant when it is seen than when
it is heard. We forget that language is primarily sounds, and that sounds
existed long before visual signs were invented.

Thus, many people still believe that there are only five vowel
sounds because there are only five vowel letters. Some teachers are
convinced that ' Austrian armies awfully arrayed ' shows an analogous
phonetic pattern to ' Boldly by batteries besieged Belgrade '. The
gimmick-form ' Rock 'n' Roll ' is considered perverse when it is merely
phonetic. A writer as sensitive to sound as J. B. Priestley can describe
the speech peculiarity of one of his characters (in *Angel Pavement*) as
follows : ' He softened all the sibilants, putting an " h " behind every
" s ".' Ivor Brown writes about ' Shakespeare's instinctive feeling for
the letter " r " ; time and time again he was to play on its emotional
vibration, especially when linked with the letter " o " '. Later he speaks
of the ' letter's potency '. This is pure Egyptian superstition. The
unwitting high priest of this cult of ' letters ' was Arthur Rimbaud, who
wrote a famous sonnet on the Vowels ; but Rimbaud was really concerned with the significance of the vowel letters in alchemy, not in
language at all.

One feels strongly that practitioners of literature should at least
show an interest in the raw material of their art. Very few do. That
awareness of the nature of sound which opens Nabokov's *Lolita* is

something rare in modern fiction : ' Lolita, light of my life, fire of my loins. My sin, my soul. Lo-lee-ta : the tip of the tongue making a trip of three steps down the palate to tap, at three, on the teeth. Lo. Lee. Ta.' Nabokov recognises that the two ' l 's of the name are different. It is no accident that this analytic acuteness of ear should be found in one of the most subtle and musical prose-writers of our time.

As the world shrinks and the need for every educated man and woman to know foreign languages grows more urgent, we have to devise techniques for learning them quickly and accurately. Our best beginning is an examination of the nature of language itself. There is no reason why this should be regarded as an expert study : we need no special equipment ; a laboratory is set on our shoulders. Apart from the utility of such a study, there should be in everyone a natural curiosity about the most fundamental of all social activities, a curiosity which our systems of education have done nothing to foster and everything to dull. It would be too much to say that all this is a matter of life and death ; but a verse from the Book of Judges indicates that occasionally it can be. Let this stand as our epigraph :

' Then said they unto him, Say now Shibboleth : and he said Sibboleth : for he could not frame to pronounce it right. Then they took him, and slew him at the passages of Jordan.'

2

No society, whether human or animal, can exist without communication. Thoughts, desires, appetites, orders these have to be conveyed from one brain to another, and they can rarely be conveyed directly. Only with telepathy do we find mind speaking straight to mind, without the intermediacy of signs, and this technique is still strange enough to seem a music-hall trick or a property of science fiction. The vast majority of sentient beings—men, women, cats, dogs, bees, horses— have to rely on signals, symbols of what we think and feel and want, and these signals can assume a vast variety of forms. There is, indeed, hardly any limit to the material devices we can use to express what is in our minds : we can wave our hands, screw up our faces, shrug our shoulders, write poems, write on walls, carve signs out of stone or wood, mould signs with clay or butter, scrawl sky-signs with an aircraft, semaphore, heliograph, telephone, run a pirate radio transmitter, stick pins in dolls. A dog will scratch at a door if it wants to be let in ; a cat

will mew for milk ; a hostess will ring a bell for the course to be
changed ; a pub-customer will rap with a coin for service ; a wolf will
whistle ; the people in the flat upstairs will bang with a stick if our
party is too noisy. One can fill pages with such examples, bringing in
the language of flowers and the signalling devices of honey-bees, but
one will always end up with human speech as the most subtle, comprehensive, and exact system of communication we possess.

And yet even this, which seems self-evident, will be questioned by
experts in other fields of communication. The musical composer will
contend that his art can go deeper and wider than words. We are moved
by music in ways that words cannot describe, and such emotion can
drive us to action—war, murder, love, religion. There is obviously
a sort of communication in music which digs down to unconscious levels
of the mind, hardly as yet understood, and this special communication
of art is one of man's most incredible activities. We cannot deny the
width of appeal that music possesses : the man in Stoke-on-Trent may
not be able to read Pushkin, but Tchaikovsky can move him to tears ;
Benjamin Britten speaks louder than W. H. Auden. But speech has
a more general usefulness, and art—whether it be music, poetry,
painting, drama, or ballet—makes up only a small part of the total life
of a society. Without speech, and the various notations of speech,
human society would not be possible at all.

Having lauded one sign-system in particular, let us return to signs in
general. These can take two main forms which, as with most opposed
things, can shade gently into each other : they can be *conventional* or
they can be *iconic*. ' Iconic ' derives from the Greek word for an image,
and it is supposed that most primitive human signs try to present
a universally recognisable image of the thought or desire which the
signaller wishes to communicate. Thus, if we are in a foreign country
and cannot speak the language, we can show hunger by going through
the motions of putting something into our mouths and then pretending
to chew. This is iconic. The phrase ' I'm hungry ' is only understood
by those who know English : a convention long established is that these
sounds stand for this particular human need, and the convention has
to be specially learned. An intelligent cat, like the Siamese I once had,
will show that it wants milk by licking an empty saucer. This seems to
be a piece of iconic signalling : the sign is an image of the fulfilment of
a need. What can we say of the sign often used in ballet or mime to

indicate love—the hands over the heart ? Is this conventional or iconic ? In a sense it overlaps both categories, for, though we no longer believe that the heart as a physical organ is the seat of love, yet we accept for the moment that the old crude anatomy of the passions is correct : within a conventional acceptance the sign then becomes iconic. And so with the transfixed heart of the Valentine. But if choreographers decide between themselves that a slap on the thigh shall indicate love, then that is a purely arbitrary symbol, a pure piece of conventional signalling.

The conventional and the iconic appear in all the arts, though the terms ' representational ' and ' non-representational ' are better known. Painting and sculpture are expected to be iconic : we are disappointed if we do not get, in however distorted a manner, a recognisable image of a person or thing. Music is nearly always a language of conventional signs (whose ' meaning ' perhaps only the unconscious mind can recognise), but with composers like Richard Strauss there is a strong iconic urge. In Strauss's symphonic poem *Don Quixote* we can hear horns imitating the bleating of sheep ; a wind machine gives us pure wind. The same instrument appears in Vaughan Williams's *Sinfonia Antartica* to represent the howling of Antarctic gales. This kind of iconic composing is rare and it is frequently condemned for its alleged crudity, but no composer faced with setting the words ' He ascended into Heaven ' is likely to make his vocal line move downwards.

Human speech is essentially a system of conventional signs, though theorists like Max Müller once held that all language sprang out of a desire to imitate natural phenomena (this was called the ' Bow-wow ' theory). There are, in all languages, many words which attempt an image of the things they represent, just as the child's word ' quack-quack ', meaning ' duck ', is an image of the duck's characteristic noise. ' Splash ' sounds like water, ' frou-frou ' sounds like the rustle of skirts. ' Pop ' is right for the bursting of a balloon, and ' boom ', however feebly, suggests a bomb going off. Even with purely visual images, it is possible to find a certain appositeness in the forms of words, though often only the linguist can explain the appositeness. Take ' moon ', for instance. Latin and its derivatives, as well as Russian, have a *lun*-form, and Malay has *bulan*. It is the u-sound which is descriptive : the lips have to imitate a moon-shape in order to give the right quality

to the tongue-sound ; the back of the tongue is raised high, very close
to the palate (which Malay, incidentally, calls the ' sky ' of the mouth),
and this seems to suggest that the moon is something high up. A word
like ' little ' seems apt, for the i-sound is made by narrowing the
passage between the front of the tongue and the palate, suggesting that
only something very little could creep through. To give the impression
of even greater littleness, the form ' leetle ' is sometimes roguishly
used : the ee-sound is even higher than the i-sound, making the space
between tongue and palate only big enough for something microscopic
to crawl through ; with ' teeny-weeny ' we are on the borders of
invisibility.

But this class of iconic words is so small as to be virtually negligible.
In any case, some very important words—the structural words like
' of ', ' if ', ' when ', ' so '—can never have had a corresponding image
in the outside world. Language is arbitrary, conventional, and has been
so from the beginning ; only the poet can invent a Golden Age of
iconic language. The device of onomatopoeia—sound imitating sense—
is beloved of lyric poets like Keats (' The murmurous haunt of flies on
summer eves ') and Tennyson (' The moan of doves in immemorial
elms '), but there are severe limits to what it can do. It is what it
tries to do that is important, and ' conventional language striving to be
iconic ' might be added to the already innumerable definitions of poetry.

But one cannot doubt that the earliest attempts to represent words
by visual signs were iconic. Chinese symbols still show, in varying
degrees of clarity, ancient attempts to *draw* the referent of the word
(that is, the thing in the outside world which the word represents), and,
when this direct representation failed, to use metaphor for rendering
the abstract concrete. And so with Egyptian picture-writing, which is
full of recognisable lions, gods, snakes, birds, water-pots. Our own
alphabet (as we shall see in a later chapter) is ultimately derived from
hieroglyphics, but all picture elements have long disappeared : the
essence of the alphabetic method is its conventionality. Only in the
letter O, which seems to come from an Egyptian drawing of an eye, do
we find anything approaching an iconic purpose : the letter represents
the shape of the mouth when pronouncing the o-sound ; here is the
' moon ' business in reverse.

An alphabet is a series of signs representing signs. The sounds I make
when saying ' man ' stand for something in the outside world ; the

letters which make up MAN stand for those sounds. Thus, with a visual system of representation, we are two removes from reality. We are three removes from reality when we use a system like Braille or Morse : the dots and dashes or embossed symbols stand for alphabetic letters ; the alphabetic letters stand for sounds ; the sounds stand for what exists in the mind or in the outside world. It is as well to stay as close to reality as possible ; that is why the study of language is a study of sounds and what sounds can do.

3

WHY and how and when did man start using those sounds which we call human language ? We can only guess. The Garden-of-Eden picture of Adam solemnly and deliberately naming everything is misleading : it assumes, like the myth of Genesis itself, a sudden act of creation after an infinite silence. Primitive man may have communicated with visual signs before he developed into a talker, but there is no reason to suppose that his meaningful movements of hands, face, and body were accompanied by silence ; he was probably very far from being a mere dumb gesticulator, a sort of silent Tarzan film. I imagine early human society as full of noise—babblings and lallings and gurglings, diversified with grunts and howls—though such noise might be a mere by-product of tongue and lip movements corresponding to the movements of bodily gesture. It is helpful to think of the present relationship of speech and gesture in reverse. We all use nods, shrugs, arm-movements, smiles, frowns, to help out speech ; perhaps primitive man used sound to help out gesture. When sound became genuine speech it had probably already shown its potential usefulness through the pleasure-principle : speech is pleasant in itself, as children know ; the exercise of the vocal organs can give delight without expressing meaning. Speech might also be an invaluable means of establishing and maintaining social contact in the event of the speaker being cut off from his fellows. Bodily gesture has a very limited visual range : trees, stones, whole forests, whole hills may get in the way of it ; darkness will render it quite useless. Speech is magical : it is powerful though invisible ; it is light in darkness.

Let us examine these two aspects of speech—speech as a medium of pleasure ; speech as a medium of contact when tactile or visual signals cannot operate. The first—the sheer joy or even elation in the use of speech—is not merely a cradle pleasure to be outgrown ; it is the basis of song and poetry. Most literary artists are tempted sometimes to concentrate on word-pattern for its own sake rather than word-pattern as a signal of meaning. The words of a poem come first ; the meaning later, even not at all. ' Take care of the sounds, and the sense will take care of itself.' Surrealism has a fair ancestry. The nonsense-poem, the hey-nonny-no lyric, the pleasures of double-talk, the delight in strange or invented words : condemnation of these by no-nonsense, say-what-you-mean-sir Gradgrinds misses one very important, though non-utilitarian, point about language. All art springs from delight in raw material ; to play with the raw material of literature is a natural pleasure linking us with a remote era that had speech but no language, but was perhaps finding language through delight in speech.

The second aspect of speech is social rather than aesthetic, though it also has little to do with ' meaning ' as we understand that term. Speech is still a means of establishing or maintaining contact with other members of society ; it serves the pure social instinct of wanting to feel oneself part of a group. Malinowski, the anthropologist, used the term *phatic communion* to describe this kind of speech activity. (The Greek root of ' phatic ' means ' show ; indicate '.) Talk about the weather rarely indicates much real interest in the weather : it is just something to say, a means of making contact or showing friendliness. Phrases like ' Roll on Death, and let's have a go at the angels ', ' Never mind, lads, it'll soon be Christmas ', ' Put another pea in the pot and hang the expense ', ' Ah, well, as one door shuts another door closes '—these may seem pointless, feeble, silly, but, as any serviceman knows, they are the warm and comfortable stuff of human companionship. (Incidentally, they belong to strong-rooted regional speech more than to deracinated Standard English). Speech to promote human warmth : that is as good a definition as any of the phatic aspect of language. For good or ill, we are social creatures and cannot bear to be cut off too long from our fellows, even if we have nothing really to say to them. We can feel strongly for primitive man in the dark ; for all our science, we have not really overcome our fear of it or, when human contact is lost, our sense of devastating loneliness in it. If we are walking, late and alone, on a dark country road, and we hear another human being approaching, we are instinctively drawn to the uttering of a few friendly meaningless words. Primitive man, separated from his fellows in the big incomprehensible blackness, must have chattered incessantly to keep contact alive.

Phatic communion, like pleasure in language for its own sake, has a great deal to do with the making of literature (which, after all, may be regarded primarily as a non-informative medium of human contact). The babbling and bubbling of Elizabethan stage-clowns goes along with the puns and the Euphuisms ; the garrulousness of pamphleteers like Nashe and Greene is more phatic than meaningful. The products of our Golden Age of literature seem the natural expression of life in a small, warm, compact, very human society—that of Shakespeare's London. What was once the heart of culture no longer produces culture ; it merely markets it. It is a huge depersonalised abstraction, no longer a society at all. Literature, as cities grow, becomes increasingly an expression of loneliness and exile—a cry in the dark, whistling in the dark.

Out of the babbling and chattering of primitive man, something like language as we know it was eventually to crystallise. We tend to think of the making of language as deliberately architectural—blueprint grammar, a dictionary-load of bricks. This is partly because of the Genesis myth and partly because of the way in which we learn foreign languages : we start off with a silence, then we try to fill the silence by learning words. We think, in fact, of the conscious creation of a structure out of verbal atoms : our unit is the smallest possible verbal form. But the unit of primitive man would be much more like a phrase, a clause, a total statement. He would learn to associate a segment of the flow of speech with a particular experience to be described or expressed. When we see a sunrise, we instinctively analyse into particles : sun, east, sky, red, gold, rising. Primitive man would see the process as a single experience, indivisible. The analytical faculty comes very late in the evolution of mankind. The isolation of the word, the breaking down of language into the stuff of grammars and dictionaries, belongs to the last few centuries. The Romans are, comparatively speaking, our near neighbours in time, but they lacked the analytical equipment to dissect their language as Hillard and Botting and Kennedy have dissected it. They did not think in terms of accusatives and gerunds and subjunctives and the principle parts of irregular verbs ; they had to accept the complex of Latin as it was.

Primitive language, then, must not be thought of as a sort of pidgin— ' him house belong me '—with words like painful little barks all separated out. 'They will be loved' is the English for the Latin *amabuntur*. The English way (and English is a progressive, self-simplifying language) is to analyse a complex experience into irreducible particles : four words to the one of the Latin. Old languages—like Sanskrit, Greek, Latin—are *synthetic* : they build up long words and do everything with inflexions or endings. We all remember *mensa, mensa, mensam, mensae, mensae, mensa*—the various inflexions of the singular form of the Latin word for a table. Modern languages tend to be *analytic*. We have an unchanging singular form 'table', and we express relationships by means of additional words : 'to a table', 'with a table,' and so on. The oldest languages of all must have been highly synthetic—verb-forms and noun-forms a mile long.

We have seen that language satisfies man in two ways—it can be pleasant in itself ; it can be a device for social contact. But we would all accept that the really important purpose of language—the *use* of language—is to convey wishes, thoughts, and feelings from one person to another, or from a person to a group, or from a group to a person, or from a group to a group. Our highly complex modern societies depend on the precise functioning of such communication. But, as science and technology develop, it becomes more and more evident that language is not precise enough. Mathematicians and engineers rely on signals capable of cold, single, unambiguous meanings ; words tend to ambiguity and vagueness—in every serious discussion much time has to be spent in re-defining common terms like 'love', 'justice', 'freedom'. Language has, in fact, many of the qualities possessed by human beings themselves—it tends to be emotional when pure reason is required, it tends to be unsure of what it means, it tends to change form, meaning, and pronunciation. It is slippery, elusive, hard to fix, define, delimit.

So, when we talk about a language—English, French, Russian, Sanskrit—we refer to a process rather than to a thing. English consists of its future as well as its past and present, and when we discuss any English word we are talking of things not yet known. A language consists of potentialities whose nature we can only guess at, though its genetic qualities help to determine its development. But, if we try to grasp the flow of the language at that non-existent point called 'now', we are still in the dark as to its boundaries, and we cannot be sure of its content. How many words are there in English ? We cannot say. It is not enough to point to the number of words in a dictionary, because no

dictionary—however large—can pretend to be complete, nor can
a dictionary take in all the various derivatives of a word. Fresh words
are being made every day ; borrowing from other languages goes
on incessantly. If, in my own home, my family uses invented words
like *shlerp*, *focklepoff*, and *arpworthy*, we are entitled to regard these
as part of English (they certainly belong to no other language, and
yet they are recognisable linguistic forms) just as *chortle*, *brillig*, and
abnihilise belong to English. It is best to regard the language as
a growing corpus of words and structures which nobody can know
entirely but upon which anybody can draw at any time—a sort of
unlimited bank account. It is not just the sum total of what has been
spoken and written ; it is also what *can* be spoken and written. It is
actual and potential. In another sense, it is a code, always ready for
individual acts of encoding.

The difficulty in linguistic study is a difficulty of balance. We have
the language itself ; we have the *idiolect*, or sum-total of any one
person's linguistic actions and linguistic potential ; we have the single
speech-act. The general pulls one way and the particular another ; the
potential and the actual are hard to juggle with ; language is seen as
a warm and living thing and also as an abstraction. We must keep our
heads, remembering W. B. Yeats's words : ' I made it out of a mouthful
of air.' He was referring to the creation of a poem ; we refer to language,
in which an infinitude of poems awaits realisation. Let us forget our
big words and vast potentials and start with a mouthful of air—the
simplest thing imaginable ; let us see what a mouthful of air can do.

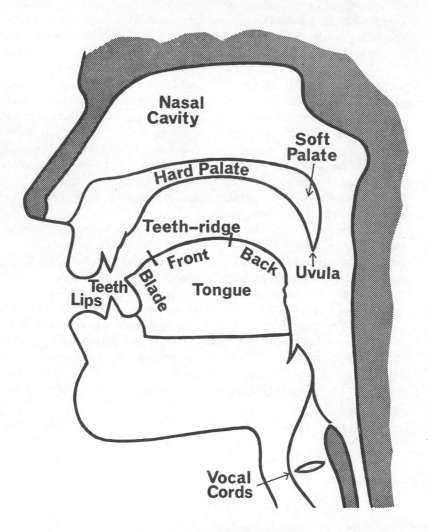

THE ORGANS OF SPEECH

TWO

THE INSTRUMENTS OF SPEECH

1

PHONETICS, 'the science of speech,' was glamourised in Shaw's *Pygmalion*, and has more recently been super-glamourised in *My Fair Lady*. Since Professor Higgins, phoneticians have seemed the most human of all scientists, and their weird way of writing down sounds ('That ain't proper writing', says Eliza Doolittle) more intriguing than forbidding. But, since Shaw wrote the play which was designed to show what important people speech-specialists are, Phonetics has become more than a matter of wandering streets with a notebook : it has drawn on the helper-sciences of electronics and statistics and erected massive laboratories. In this chapter, and the two that follow, we shall nevertheless content ourselves with the laboratory that our speech-mechanism provides, 'a mouthful of air,' and a few special phonetic symbols. Our purpose is, after all, a very humble one : we merely want to understand the *elements* of speech.

Before we go any further, we have to distinguish two separate kinds of speech-study. The first is *Phonetics*, which examines speech-sounds without direct reference to how these are used in language. It is interested in the mechanics and acoustics of speech, and it rejoices in the endless variety of sounds that are possible to the human mouth. The other study is called *Phonology*, or *Phonemics*, and it relates speech-sounds directly to their linguistic function. Let us make all this clear with an example. Pronounce the words 'cool', 'kill', and 'keel'. You would agree, I think, that they all begin with a k-sound. (Ignore the spelling. If we have 'k' before 'o', 'u', or 'a', we represent the k-sound with a 'c'. This is a mere spelling convention.) Pronounce the words again ; pronounce them several times. You will discover that the three k-sounds are not exactly alike. They are all recognisably k-sounds, but for 'cool' the k-sound is made a little further back in the mouth than for the k-sounds of the other two words. And the k-sound in 'keel' is a little nearer the teeth than is the k-sound in 'kill'. It seems, then, that there is a general class of k-sound and that this can be divided into species. The general class, the k-family, is called a *phoneme*, and the types of k-sound within the family are called *allophones*. Experiment with other groups of words, like ' tar ', ' ten ', and ' tea ', and you will find the same principle applying. The three t-sounds are different from each other, but they all belong to the same t-family : they are allophones of the t-phoneme.

The phonologist, the man who is concerned with phonemes, is not greatly concerned with the sub-division of the phoneme into allophones. To him, the phoneme is the speech-unit. He knows that it is not possible to pronounce the k-sound of ' cool ' in ' kill ' or ' keel ' ; he knows that if we pronounce the l-sound at the end of ' cool ' in place of the l-sound at the beginning of ' look ' we are not going to alter the meaning of the word. The two l-sounds are different, as you can verify for yourself : they are allophones of the l-phoneme. But the difference is not a significant one : it makes no *semantic* alteration (' semantic ' is the word we use when we are talking about ' meaning ') in the utterance. But to the phonetician, these divisions of the phoneme are of great interest : the atomisation of ' k ' or ' l ' or ' t ' into its allophonic constituents is the primal joy of the phonetician. Every single possible human sound falls within his province, and he cares nothing for the linguistic function—the ' meaning '—of these sounds.

In studying speech-sounds either phonetically or phonologically, we have to equip ourselves with a precise means of notating them : we need a special alphabet, though the phonetician needs a bigger one (one with more letters) than the phonologist. The need for a special alphabet is made clear when we consider the limitations of our ordinary everyday one—the alphabet which is capable of using the same letter for the different o-sounds of ' not ', ' note ', ' woman ', and ' women '. The difficulties we would encounter if we had to rely on the ordinary Roman alphabet for a study of the English vowel-sounds are best seen in the following sentence. This contains all the English vowel-sounds. Pronounce it in a mechanical, zombie-like way, giving every word the same importance, the same stress. For ' AND ', though, use the slack sound used for the apostrophe before the ' n ' in ' Rock 'n' Roll '.

WHO WOULD KNOW AUGHT OF ART MUST LEARN, ACT, AND
  1   2   3   4   5 6   7   8   9 10

THEN TAKE HIS EASE.
11   12   13   14

Isolate the vowel-sounds, and we have the following :

O	OU	OW	AU	O	A	U	EA	A	A	E	A-E	I	EA
1	2	3	4	5	6	7	8	9	10	11	12	13	14

This is at once seen to be hopelessly inadequate. That is why we use the symbols of the International Phonetic Association (the International Phonetic Alphabet or IPA), which is accepted and understood wherever language scholars meet. Symbols of the IPA * will, in this book, be placed between oblique lines, so that the above vowel-sounds are notated as follows :

/uː/	/ʊ/	/oʊ/	/ɔː/	/ɒ/	/ɑː/	/ʌ/	/ɜː/	/æ/	/ə/
1	2	3	4	5	6	7	8	9	10

/ɛ/	/eɪ/	/ɪ/	/iː/
11	12	13	14

Note that Nos. 1, 4, 6, 8, 14 consist of a letter followed by a colon (:). This colon indicates that the vowel-sound is long : it actually takes longer to pronounce No. 1 than No. 2, longer to pronounce No. 4 than No. 5. Note also that Nos. 3 and 12 do not consist of single letters but of two letters. These are *diphthongs* or double sounds : they represent a journey made by the tongue from the position for the first vowel towards the position for the second vowel. English is very rich in diphthongs :

FEAR	THE	POOR	OUTSIDE	THE	DOOR.	BEWARE	OF
1		2	3	4		5	6

POWER ;	AVOID	DESIRE.
7	8	9

/ɪə/	/ʊə/	/aʊ/	/aɪ/	/ɔə/	/ɛə/
1	2	3	4	5	6

/aʊə/	/ɔɪ/	/aɪə/
7	8	9

Note that Nos. 7 and 9 of this group are *triphthongs* or three-fold sounds : the journey made by the tongue to encompass the diphthong /aɪ/ or /aʊ/ has an extra lap added, and this ends up in the middle of the

---

* The symbols used in this book belong to the *narrow* notational system of the International Phonetic Alphabet. For a comparison between this and the *broad* system, see Appendix One. The narrow system has more symbols and hence is more accurate than the broad.

mouth with the slack neutral vowel /ə/ (the vowel of the second syllable of ' father ', ' mother ', ' sister ', ' brother '.).

There is no need to plunge into learning the symbols of the IPA. We shall meet them singly and without fuss in the course of our survey of speech-sounds. It is enough, for the moment, to recognize their usefulness.

2

WE come now to the organs of speech. Speech-sounds are made out of out-breathed air. This air is moulded into different shapes, obstructed and then released, or allowed to escape to the outer atmosphere under pressure. In other words, the air from our lungs is modified by the various organs that lie in the throat and mouth. We can take it as a near-invariable rule that speech is made from out-breathed air, though certain African languages use an in-breathed (' imploded ') sound— /m/ or /n/—at the beginning of some words. In the name ' Mboya ' we start off with an in-breathed /m/.

In the upper part of the windpipe lies the *larynx* (or Adam's apple), which contains and protects the *vocal cords*. The vocal cords resemble a pair of lips. Stretched across the larynx, from front to back, they are tough pieces of membrane capable of coming together and then separating again. The space between them is called the *glottis* (the Greek word for ' voice '), but it is really the cords themselves that constitute the voice. Air makes them vibrate, and this vibration is the rich musical sound we hear in song. The vibration of the vocal cords is not enough in itself to provide richness, any more than a violin string removed from the violin-body can give as much more than a thin screech. Voice requires resonators, like any musical instrument, and resonance is given by the chest, the throat, the mouth-cavity and nose-cavity, and the sinuses. These hollows of various sizes magnify the fundamental sound produced by the voice.

We can, then, bring the vocal cords together (it is a process we can learn to do consciously) in the same way that we can bring our lips together. The out-breathed air coming from the lungs forces its way through the two membranes and makes them vibrate. This vibration goes on when we pronounce a vowel-sound or when we articulate a consonant such as /b/, /d/, /m/, /z/. (These phonetic symbols have the same value as in the ordinary alphabet.) These sounds, made with the vocal cords brought together and vibrating away with the impact of air from the lungs, are called *voiced* sounds, that is, sounds made with the voice. There would not be much speech without the voice (for a start, there would be no vowels), and we have some notion of what it is like to have no voice when we are suffering from laryngitis. When the vocal cords are diseased and have to be removed, there are two ways of creating a substitute : one can learn to send up ' voiced ' air from the stomach (this is true ventriloquism or ' belly-talk ') or one can be equipped with an artificial larynx. But these medical aspects of speech really lie outside our province.

When the vocal cords are apart from each other—like parted lips— the air is allowed to come up through the windpipe without meeting any obstruction in the larynx. This gives us pure *breath*, which we hear in the English aspirate /h/. When we utter sounds like /p/, /t/, /k/, /f/, /s/, the vocal cords are wide apart, unvibrated by the air from the lungs, and we call these sounds *unvoiced* sounds. If one alternates sounds like /s/ and /z/ very rapidly, one is making the vocal cords open and shut athletically. You can tell the difference between an unvoiced sound and a voiced sound by covering your ears with your hands when you speak. If you can feel a vibration, then the sound is voiced. The vibration of the vocal cords has communicated itself to the bones of your head.

Another thing that the vocal cords can do is to come together tightly, presenting a shut double-door to the air that is clamouring to come up from below. This is known as *closed glottis*. When the vocal cords suddenly separate, the air—formerly compressed underneath— rushes out in an explosion of some violence. This effect is known as a *glottal stop* (really, of course, it is a stop followed by a release) and it is far more common in language than people realise. There is no letter for it in the ordinary Roman alphabet, and this blinds (or deafens) most of us to its existence. We can hear it in the Cockney ' Wha' a lo' of li'l bo'les ' (' What a lot of little bottles ') or in the Scotsman's ' Sa'urday '. The IPA represents it as a question mark without a dot, thus : /ʔ/.

The other vocal organs are visible in a mirror or even capable of being touched. Some are movable, as the vocal cords are ; others stay still. Let us look at the movables first. Open your mouth to a mirror, and you will see a small fleshy organ hanging at the back : this is the *uvula* (Latin for ' little grape '.) It is, as it were, a tail light attached to the *soft palate* or *velum*, and the soft palate is capable of moving down

to meet the back of the tongue or up away from it. It is a door con-
necting the mouth with the nose cavity or *nasal pharynx*, and it determines whether the air breathed out from the lungs shall escape by the
mouth or by the nostrils. If the soft palate moves up, then there is
a space between the uvula and the back of the tongue, and the air can
come into the mouth and then go out between the lips into the great
world outside. Most of the sounds we make are made with this mouth-
air. But if the soft palate moves down, so that it rests on the back of
the tongue, then the air cannot come into the mouth from the windpipe :
it meets a closed door. All it can do is to move into the nose cavity or
nasal pharynx, and then make its exit through the nostrils. The
sounds /m/, /n/, and /ŋ/ (the last sound is the ' ng ' of ' sing ') are made
by allowing the air to come out via the nose (by courtesy of the soft
palate) and are hence called *nasal* sounds. Vowels can be nasalised as
well, and the French language has a plentiful supply of nasalised vowels.
In very casual English speech nasalisation of a vowel takes the place
of a following /n/. I knew a man who habitually entered a pub with
the one word /pɑ̃ː/ . . . (The little sign called a *tilde* that appears over
the /ɑː/ signifies nasalisation.) This meant ' Pint '. Over the years this
man had simplified the word in the following stages : (1) /paɪnt/
(2) /paɪn/ (3) /pãĩ/ (4) /pɑ̃ː/. Children with adenoid growths—spongy
matter obstructing the passage of air into the nasal pharynx—cannot
pronounce nasal sounds and so are unable to say the following very
clearly : ' Do not be afraid, I am only the sandman, and with my bag
of golden sand I bring sleep to everyone.' What we get instead is something like ' Do dot be afraid, I ab odly the sadbad, ad with by bag of
golded sad I brig sleep to everywud '. When we have a bad cold—
mucus clogging the nasal pharynx—we have the same sort of difficulty.
For some reason this is popularly called ' speaking through one's nose ',
which is precisely what it is not.

The most lively of the movable speech-organs is the tongue, and, as
we shall see, it is by far the most important of them all : indeed
' tongue ' is a synonym for ' language ' in many languages or tongues,
and ' language ' itself derives from the Latin word for a tongue. We
can, for convenience, divide this very meaty organ into three parts—
the *blade*, including the *tip* ; the *front* ; the *back*. When the tongue is
lying at rest, the blade is opposite the ridge of the upper teeth, the front
is opposite the hard palate (or roof of the mouth), the back is opposite

the soft palate. These three parts of the tongue govern, as far as speech is concerned, these three corresponding parts of the mouth. The remaining movable organs are the lips, which are the first speech-instruments we learn to use as babies (apart, of course, from the vocal cords, which we make lusty use of as soon as we are born). Our first words are ' baba ', ' papa ', ' mama ', all based on lip-sounds.

The fixed organs are the *hard palate*, that concave, rocky, rather ticklish, dome of the mouth ; the *teeth* ; the *teeth-ridge* or *alveolum*— that convex part of the roof of the mouth which lies immediately behind the roots of the teeth.

These, then, are the agents which mould, bully, and coax our ' mouthful of air ' into speech.

3

ALMOST from the very beginning of recorded human language, it seems to have been recognised that there are two complementary elements in the total body of speech-sounds—vowels and consonants. The ancient Hebrews found the consonants earthy and the vowels heavenly, and they never allowed the latter to come down to earth and be represented alphabetically. There is no doubt something gross and brash and materialistic about consonants : they are noises made by banging things together, rubbing, hissing, buzzing. Vowels, on the other hand, are pure music—woodwind to the consonantal percussion—and, because they are produced by the creation of spaces between the tongue and the hard or soft palate, and these spaces are not measured scientifically but arrived at by a sort of guesswork, they tend to be indefinite and change-able. The history of the sound-changes of any language is mainly a history of its vowels.

Again, our difficulty in learning a foreign language is chiefly a vowel-difficulty. The problems offered by the initial and middle consonants of Mr Khrushchev's name are soon overcome. You make the kh-sound /x/ by retching briefly ; you practise on ' smashed china ' for the shch-sound (щ in the Russian alphabet ; /ʃtʃ/ in the IPA). But to make the u-sound (/y/) in French *lune* or German *über* requires a complete reorientation of vowel-habits : we have, to put it technically, to change our phonemic thinking. In our brief survey of speech-sounds, we can dispose of consonants quickly and gaily enough ; vowels are a different matter. Consonants first, then.

B

TABLE OF CONSONANTS AND SEMI-VOWELS

	Plosive		Fricative		Nasal		Lateral		Trilled		Semi-Vowel	
	U.	V.	U.	V.	U.	V.	U.	V.	U.	V.	U.	V.
Bilabial	p	b	ɸ	β	—	m	—	—	—	—	ʍ	w
Labio-dental	—	—	f	v	—	ɱ[1]	—	—	—	—	—	—
Linguo-dental	—	—	θ	ð	—	—	—	—	—	—	—	—
Dental and Alveolar	t	d	s —	z { ɹ ɹ̩	—	n	ļ	{ l ɬ	—	r r	—	—
Palatal	—	—	ʃ	ʒ	—	ɲ	(ļ)[2] —	(l)[2] λ	—	—	ç	j
Velar	k	g	x	ɣ	—	ŋ	—	(ɬ)[2]	—	R	—	—
Glottal	ʔ	—	—	—	—	—	—	—	—	—	—	—

The above table does not give every possible consonant and semi-vowel—merely the chief ones.

U. = Unvoiced. V. = Voiced.

[1] A nasal sometimes used after /v/ in words like 'even', 'Stephen', etc.

[2] Secondary articulation (viz., what the rest of the tongue is doing while the tongue-tip is on the teeth-ridge).

THREE

BANGS, HISSES, AND BUZZES

1

Plosives

ONE way of making a consonant is to play a rather sadistic trick on the air that comes up from our lungs. We can hold it back, preventing it from reaching the world outside, and then, when it thinks it is imprisoned for ever, suddenly release it. The release is so sudden and unexpected that it is accompanied by a rather violent noise—an explosion. And so consonants of this kind are called *plosives* ; sometimes, because of their trick of stopping the air coming out of the mouth, they are called *stop consonants*.

If we close our lips tightly, imprisoning air in the mouth, then suddenly open the lips, we get the plosive consonant /p/. If we do the same thing with our vocal cords vibrating, we get the plosive consonant /b/. Remembering that the word *bilabial* means ' involving the use of both lips ', we can give these two phonemes their scientific names :

/p/—unvoiced bilabial plosive
/b/—voiced bilabial plosive

For the plosives /t/ and /d/, the stopping of the air is made by pressing the tongue-tip against the teeth-ridge or alveolum. Again, the vocal cords are open and hence not vibrating for the first phoneme of the pair ; for the second there is vibration or voice :

/t/—unvoiced alveolar plosive
/d/—voiced alveolar plosive

The use of the tongue against the alveolum is perhaps more characteristic of English than of other languages. French, Italian, Malay, for instance, prefer to bring the tongue-tip on to the teeth themselves rather than on the teeth-ridge above. The Irish, when uttering a word like ' true ' (/t/ followed by a trilled /r/), make the /t/ so very much on the teeth that, in novels and stories, their pronunciation is often rendered as ' thrue '. This difference between what we may call the English /t/ phoneme and the non-English /t/ phoneme is something to

listen for on the radio, twirling the dial with a purely phonetic purpose.
A transistor set can be a very useful portable speech laboratory.

Our third pair of plosives is made by stopping the air from the lungs
with the back of the tongue pressed against the soft palate or velum ;
the sounds made on release of the air are

/k/—unvoiced velar plosive
/g/—voiced velar plosive

There are certain subtleties and refinements involved in both the
stop and the release. Sometimes we content ourselves with the stop
and ignore the release. This always happens when two plosives follow
each other, as in ' licked ' (/kt/) or ' stopped ' (/pt/) or a phrase like
' bad boy ' (/db/) or ' good girl ' (/dg/) : with each pair of stops, only
the second is released. It is eccentric to say ' badder boy ' or ' gooder
girl ' in the belief that you are giving the consonants their ' full value '.
The average man often knows better than the elocution teacher. In
some languages there is never any release. The stop consonants of
Malay (they cannot be called plosives, for they do not explode) merely
stop the air and then let it die, as in words like *sĕdap, balek, sĕbab, kulit*.
The effect to the British ear is something like that of the glottal stop.

Unvoiced plosives in English are often very breathy—*aspirated*, in
fact, so that (and this is especially true of Lancashire speech) we hear
a definite /h/ following the /p/ in a word like ' pal ' or ' pale '. One of
my Lancashire friends, who talked of going to a pub to drink some pale
ale with his pal Percy, expended a lot of breath in the process. This
perhaps gave him a thirst. In speaking most Continental languages,
we have to tame this British forcefulness and make our plosives glide
straight on to the following vowel without any breathiness.

In some forms of English, particularly American, /t/ in the middle
of a word is changed to something approaching /d/—a sort of partially
voiced /t/, represented as /ţ/. You will hear this in words like ' water '
and ' Saturday '. Sometimes the change is more radical, so that /t/
is transformed into a weak /r/ and we hear something like ' warer ' or
' Sarurday '. The process is respectable enough (' porridge ' was once
' pottage ', from French *potage*), though it is not normally associated
with Queen's English. It is not a symptom of laziness but a result of
assimilation : the vowels that flank the /t/ are, of course, voiced sounds,
and they try to make the /ţ/ assimilate some of their voiced quality.

When they turn the /t/ into /r/ they are making it assume some of the non-percussive quality which is the characteristic of a vowel : the /r/ is, in fact, so weak as to seem to stand on the border-line of vowel and consonant.

Children often confuse plosives : they say ' tum ' for ' come ', though they are no longer as savagely punished for it as Ernest was in Samuel Butler's *The Way of All Flesh*. They also say ' bockle ' for ' bottle '. This confusion can be seen in such a word as ' apricot ', whose older (Shakespearean) form is ' apricock ', derived from the Arabic *al-precoq*, itself derived from the Latin *praecox*.

2

Nasals

THE three voiced plosives /b/, /d/, /g/ are, of course, made with mouth-air. When they are sounded through the nose (by courtesy of the soft palate, which drops to allow this to happen) we get the three common nasal sounds /m/, /n/, /ŋ/—this latter symbol standing for the ' ng ' in ' sing '. These nasals can be pronounced sharply, like plosives, in such forms as the child's ' mamamamamama ', but they can also take on the continuous quality of a vowel, as in the expression of content (a warm fire, a sofa, a box of chocolates) which can be written as ' mmmmmmmmmm '. /ŋ/ is the only one of three that never appears at the beginning of a word in Western languages, though Eastern languages are quite happy to use it initially (Malay—*ngada*, *ngap*, *ngĕri*) and Chinese has it as a word complete in itself—*Ng*. In the English of Chaucer's time it was always followed by /g/, as it still is in the North, where ' singing ' is pronounced ' singgingg '. Even in the South, teachers seem to encourage children who say ' singin' ', ' goin' ', ' talkin' ' to think that they are ' dropping their g's ' and to replace /n/ by /ŋg/. This shows the primacy of spelling over pronunciation : because people see two letters in the ordinary spelling ' ng ' they think there are really two sounds there. It is curious that the Cockney's ' singin' and dancin' ' is considered vulgar while the County's ' huntin', shootin' and fishin' ' is regarded as genteel. Anyway, so-called ' g-dropping ' is merely the substitution of one nasal (/n/) for another (/ŋ/), and its ancestry is most respectable.

When a plosive appears before a nasal an interesting phenomenon takes place. Say ' kitten ', ' garden ', ' shopman ', ' button ', and you will find that you are, as it were, exploding the /t/, /d/, or /p/ through your nose. The tongue or lips remain in the position for the plosive and the soft palate drops to let the air rush out through the nose for the nasal consonant that follows. Many people pronounce ' mutton ' and ' garden ' more or less as they are spelt, insisting on a vowel between the plosive (/t/ or /d/) and the nasal (/n/). This is finicking elocution-teacher stuff : it is best to cut down work to a minimum and let the soft palate change over from plosive to nasal without any intervening vowel. This process is known as *faucal plosion* (the fauces is the narrow passage between the soft palate and the base of the tongue).

We have already referred briefly to nasalisation and noted that one of the great phonetic characteristics of French is its tendency to nasalise vowels. This nasalisation is the result of dropping nasal consonants but allowing a nasal ghost to haunt what is left of the word. In *un*, for instance, the final *n* has long disappeared from the pronunciation, but the *u* remembers it and, as a kind of memorial tribute, nasalises itself. French is fond of dropping final sounds, but, while it is ready to forget completely the final /t/ in *restaurant*, it is always faithful to the departed nasal : the final *a* comes straight out of the nostrils.

3

Fricatives

CERTAIN consonants are made by ' rubbing ' the air-stream between two vocal organs that have been brought very close together : the root of *fricative* is the same as that of ' friction '. The effect is the same as that of gas escaping through a tiny aperture : we are aware of pressure, we are aware of duration. Fricative consonants can be continued as long as the breath lasts, and hence they are acoustically very different from plosives, which are instantaneous, gone with the wind. Let us start with the lips.

By rubbing air between the nearly closed lips we are able to make two sounds which are no longer officially English phonemes, though they are to be found in other languages. The unvoiced lip fricative is, to the English ear, like a combination of /p/, /f/, and /h/. It was a common sound in ancient Greek, and the IPA uses the old Greek letter to represent it : /φ/ (phi). The Romans heard it as an aspirated /p/ and so Latinised Greek words which contained it as *philosophia*, *Phoebe*, and so on. We, who use the Roman alphabet, continue the custom, and the very name of our present study begins with an aspirated /p/ which has become pure /f/ : Phonetics. The voiced lip fricative is represented by a kind of beta-letter : /β/. It is the sound we hear when the modern Greeks utter the name of their hero Byron (to the English ear it seems like ' Vyron ') and when the Spaniards say the *v* in *vaso*.

It seems likely that the voiced bilabial fricative (/β/) existed for a long time in colloquial English, especially that of lower-class Londoners, and that it was used indifferently where we would now use /v/ and /w/. To Charles Dickens, a great novelist who worked before descriptive linguistics had come into existence, it appeared that the two Wellers, *père et fils*, said /v/ when they meant /w/ and /w/ when they meant /v/. It seems unlikely that Mr Weller said, ' Be wery careful o' vidders all your life,' but probable that he said, ' Be /β/ery careful o' /β/idders . . .' And so, when Sam, asked whether he spelt his name with a ' V ' or a ' W ', replied, ' That depends upon the taste and fancy of the speller,' he was as good as saying that the English alphabet had no letter for the bilabial fricative /β/. Certainly, both /v/ and /w/ seem only recently to have come to the enjoyment of clear identities, though many foreigners regard them still as unnatural sounds. /v/ has no place in either Chinese or Malay ; the bilabial fricative is as common in the speech of English-speaking Orientals as it was in the speech of nineteenth-century London. /w/ puzzles most Continentals.

More familiar than the two bilabial fricatives are the *labiodental fricatives*, sounds made by pressing the upper teeth on the lower lip and allowing the air to filter through the tooth-gaps. These two phonemes are :

/f/—unvoiced labio-dental fricative
/v/—voiced labio-dental fricative

The latter sound has to be taught to Oriental students of English. The directions are simple : bite the lower lip and sing at the same time. Two fricatives that may be regarded as typically English (though they once existed in all Germanic languages and are found still in Icelandic) are those made by placing the tongue-tip between the teeth and (*a*)

blowing for the unvoiced fricative ; (*b*) singing for the voiced fricative.
The unvoiced sound is the ' th ' of ' thin ', ' thick ', ' eighth ', ' path '
and the voiced sound is the ' th ' of 'then ', ' that ', ' those ', ' them '.
We use only the one digraph (two letters) to represent the two different
phonemes in the ordinary alphabet ; this is highly confusing. In the
IPA we use the Greek letter /θ/ for the unvoiced sound, the Anglo-
Saxon (and Icelandic) letter /ð/ for the voiced sound, thus :

/θ/—unvoiced linguo-dental·fricative, as in ' thin '
/ð/—voiced linguo-dental fricative, as in ' then '

The voiced linguo-dental fricative is found in Welsh disguised as *dd*
(*gorwedd ; cerdded*) ; an approach to it is made in some Spanish words,
such as *madre*, where the *d* is articulated almost on the points of the
upper teeth. Castilian Spanish (*not* South American) has /θ/, represented, before *i* or *e*, by *c*, as in the name Cervantes, or else by *z*, as in
lapiz or *luz*. Yet the two phonemes are regarded by many foreigners
as typically English eccentricities, and the pretence goes on in many
a classroom abroad that they are hard to learn.

English-speaking children and members of the Edwardian aristocracy
traditionally have difficulty with these two phonemes : inability to say
them is called *thetatismus*, but the cause of this is usually less mechanical
than acoustic. To many ears they sound like allophones of /f/ and /v/
respectively, and this is particularly true of speech in the East End of
London, where they tend to ask the riddle ' How many fevvers on
a frush's froat ? ' and get the answer ' Five fousand free hundred and
firty-free '. Yet such speakers do not lack the mechanical equipment
to make the two sounds : they have teeth, they have tongues. It
is a matter of their not finding /θ/ and /ð/ significant or ' phonemic '.

A pair of fricatives made by putting the tongue-tip on the alveolum
and rubbing the air-stream between gives us a near-universal hiss (/s/)
and buzz (/z/)—the unvoiced and voiced alveolar fricatives. Spanish
possesses the letter ' z ' but not the phoneme /z/ ; German avoids /s/
whenever it can, pronouncing words like *Sohn* and *Sommer* with a /z/.
English has a healthy distribution of both phonemes, but it hates
representing /z/ phonetically, even where usage allows this. Many
people consider spellings like ' civilized ' uncivilised ; they agree with
Shakespeare that ' whoreson zed ' is an ' unnecessary letter '. This is
a pity. The spellings ' cloze ' and ' close ' would distinguish two different

words; 'boyz' and 'girlz' would be helpful to English-learning foreigners.

Let us now give the point of the tongue a rest and place the *front* of the tongue on the hard palate (a piece of meat on an inverted butcher's slab) and squeeze the air-stream between. This gives us our two palatal consonants—the sound in 'fish', 'shell', 'passion', which is unvoiced; the sound in 'pleasure', 'leisure', French *je, jamais*, which is voiced:

/ʃ/—unvoiced palatal fricative ('sh')
/ʒ/—voiced palatal fricative ('zh')

These two sounds are often substituted by drunks for the corresponding alveolar fricatives /s/ and /z/. ('Yesh, that'sh absholutely true, conshtable. I wazh jusht shnatching a little shnoozhe in the front sheat.') This is because less delicacy of control is required to articulate with the front of the tongue than with the tip of the tongue, and drunkenness does not admit of much delicacy.

/ʃ/ is common enough in English, but /ʒ/ is very rare and never found at the beginning of a word. Two far more common phonemes consist of combinations of these two sounds with plosive consonants, thus: /tʃ/; /dʒ/. The first one is heard in words like 'chicken', 'cheat', 'catch', 'bitch', 'fetch' and 'kitchen'; the second one appears as 'j' in words like 'joke', 'John', 'jam', 'jelly', as 'g' in 'gentle', 'gin', 'pigeon', and as 'dge' in words like 'dodge', 'wedge', 'gadget'.

This combination of a plosive with a fricative is a feature of English well worth examining. The plosive, instead of terminating in an explosion, allows the two articulating organs to separate gradually, so that we hear a near-by fricative. /tʃ/ and /dʒ/ are not the only examples of this; we have also /tθ/ in 'eighth', /dθ/ in 'width', /ts/ in 'bets', /dz/ in 'beds'. The form (plosive ending in a fricative) is known as an *affricate*. The only two affricates we associate with the beginning, as well as the middle and end, of an English word are /tʃ/ and /dʒ/, but various regional forms of English substitute /ts/ for /t/ in words like 'too', 'ten', 'tell'. (I have just seen a television commercial in which a young housewife praises a detergent. Her last words are 'Keeps my hands pretty, /ts/oo.'') /dz/ sometimes appears instead of /d/. I have heard 'Drop /dz/ead'. The 'Z' in German words like ' *Zeche* ', ' *Zeug* ', ' *Ziel* ' is a /ts/. In German words that have the same origin as certain English words this /ts/ is equivalent to English /s/ (*Zelle* = ' cell ') or English /t/ (*zu* = ' to ' or ' too ').

We move to the soft palate and the back of the tongue for our last fricatives. If the back of the tongue rubs against the soft palate (or velum), without any vibration of the vocal cords, then we have the fricative heard in German or Welch *Bach* or Scottish *loch*. The Greeks had a letter for this sound (χ), and we remember this when we represent it phonetically as /x/. The Russians use ' X ' for it : it is the first sound of Mr Khrushchev's name. The ' X ' of our abbreviation ' Xmas ' commemorates the Greek spelling of Christ's name (*Χρίστος*). The ' ch ' which the Romans used to represent the Greek velar fricative (' chorus ', ' chaos ') shows that they thought the sound to be a sort of aspirated /k/. This sound is not so outlandish : all the Celtic languages have it and most of the Germanic ones. Arabic and Malay use it as well as Russian. The voiced version of the velar fricative is less common. It is a gargling noise found in Arabic and, with some German speakers, at the end of words like *Pfennig, Honig, Leipzig*. Here is the IPA symbol for it : /g/.

/x/—unvoiced velar fricative
/g/—voiced velar fricative

4

Different Kinds of L

THE consonants we have glanced at so far are fairly straightforward in the way they are articulated and the way they jet out the air from mouth or nose. The L-sound is rather more mysterious. Primarily, it is made by stopping mouth-air with the tip of the tongue against the teeth-ridge and allowing the air to sneak out along one or both sides of the tongue. For this reason, /l/ is called a *lateral* consonant. Sometimes, because the air-stream can be divided into two separate side-currents, it is also called a *divided* consonant.

The /l/ phoneme in English has two distinct allophones. (I had better qualify this statement at once by saying *British* English.) The /l/ we hear before vowels or after consonants has a thin, clear quality, suggesting somehow the resonance of the vowel /iː/ in ' see '. Listen to it : ' light ' ; ' long ' ; ' lean ' ; ' flight ' ; ' cling ' ; ' clean '. It is usually called ' clear L ', and it is the /l/ we hear in every possible position in French, Italian, Spanish, German words. But there is another kind of /l/—the one we hear in ' tell ' ; ' ale ' ; ' fall ' ; ' milk ' ; ' talc ' ; ' film ' : in other words, the /l/ that comes after a vowel and before a consonant. This is called ' dark L '. What makes them sound different ?

Here we have to use some heavy technical language. In the first place, let us write them down in the symbols provided by the IPA. /l/ is the phoneme ; |l| is the allophone known as ' clear L ' ; |ł| is the allophone known as ' dark L '. (Note that we use vertical lines to enclose allophonic symbols.) Both have a *primary* articulation of tongue-tip against teeth-ridge ; but they also have a *secondary* articulation, and this is what makes them sound different. With |l|, the front of the tongue is raised towards the hard palate : ' clear L ' is a *palatalised* sound. With |ł|, the back of the tongue is raised towards the soft palate : ' dark L ' is a *velarised* sound.

Most dialects of British English (Tyneside is one exception that springs to mind) use both the clear and dark varieties. American English tends to use only ' dark L ', which gives transatlantic speech one of its special peculiarities. When we are learning most foreign languages, it is safe to assume that the ' clear ' variety of /l/ is in use wherever the letter ' l ' appears. What makes French *ville* different from English ' veal ' is partly the length of the vowel, but chiefly the quality of the l-sound (' clear ' in French, ' dark ' in English). We can represent the French word as /vil/, the English word as /viːł/.

' Dark L ' sometimes becomes so dark in English that it changes into a vowel. I have heard Cockneys pronounce /miłk/ as /miok/. With some words, the ' dark L ' becomes the semi-vowel /w/, so that ' eels ' is pronounced not as /iːłz/ but as /iwz/. Sometimes the ' dark L ' grows so obscure that it disappears entirely. This has happened in Queen's English in words like ' walk ', ' talk ', ' palm ', ' calm '.

Both ' clear ' and ' dark ' L are *voiced* sounds : the vocal cords vibrate steadily while they are being uttered. Welsh has the distinction of possessing an *unvoiced* l-sound, one of the distinguishing badges of the language ; Welsh spells this sound consistently as *ll*. It is found in such common names as Llanelly, Llewelyn, Llandudno, and the near-rude place-name that Dylan Thomas invented—Llareggyb. It is an insult to a noble language to ignore this special Welsh phoneme and treat it as an allophone of the English /l/. Unvoiced L, which the IPA represents as /l̥/, is an easy enough sound to learn. Put your tongue in the position for 'clear L' and blow instead of singing. Or, in other words, aspirate your /l/. There is no need to take special lessons in Cardiff or Ynys Ddu.

5

Different Kinds of R

IT is proper to consider the various r-sounds immediately after examining /l/ and its sister /l̥/. The fates of 'l' and 'r' have often been closely linked in the history of language. Western people expect the Chinese to say 'flied lice' for 'fried rice' (some, but not all, do). The Malay word for 'English' is *Inggĕris*. Insulting prison-camp Japanese would say 'broody' for 'bloody'. 'Glamour' is derived from the Middle English 'gramarye', meaning nothing more glamorous than 'grammar'. 'Flagellation' comes from Latin *flagellum*, which is a diminutive of *flagrum* (' a whip'). *Blanco* ('white') in Spanish is *branco* in Portuguese. It would seem that both L and R have something of the indefinite quality of a vowel and, where they do not change into vowels, they are sometimes willing to change into each other.

That the English r-sound is generally ready to change from caterpillar-consonant to vowel-butterfly is shown in a very great number of words : 'here', 'there', 'father', 'park', 'shirt' are just a few. The 'r', in a final or near-final position in English, can turn into a 'slack' vowel-sound like /ə/ or /ɜː/ ('here' = /hɪə/ ; 'shirt' = /ʃɜ·t/) or a lengthener of the preceding vowel (/park/ has become /pɑ·k/). (Note that a long vowel is only half-long—a single dot instead of a full colon—before an unvoiced consonant.) The English r-sound is, in fact, a very weak fricative, so weak that it can hardly stand upright and is, indeed, an upside-down symbol in the IPA : /ɹ/. This is the usual sound we hear at the beginning of English words like 'right', 'rose', 'wrong' in most parts of the country. The point of the tongue curls up a little and engages the hard palate.

The Americans and Irish have not allowed the r-sound in words like 'hard', 'girl', 'mother' and the rest to disappear completely. They make the tongue-tip curl up considerably—a kind of back-twisting movement which is called *retroflex*—and this gives us the obscure sound we represent as /ɹ/. But, in a great deal of American pronunciation, we get the impression that the tongue is curling up without engaging the palate, and that the vowel that comes before the ' r ' in words like ' are ', ' dark ', and so on is pronounced merely with the tongue in a retroflex position. An Englishman will say /pɜːɫ/ for ' pearl ', but an American is likely to say either /pɜːɹɫ/ or /pɝːɫ/, the dot in the latter transcription signifying that the tongue is curled up or ' retroflex ' while the vowel is being uttered. Our two kinds of r-sound so far, then, may be tabulated as follows :

/ɹ/—fricative ' r '

/ɻ/—retroflex or ' inverted ' fricative ' r '

One may note before passing on to further types of r-sound that it is traditional for babies and members of the aristocracy in old-type films or stories to have difficulty in pronouncing ' r ' and to substitute for it either /w/—as in a ' wed, wed wose '—or the bilabial fricative /β/. This is regarded, somewhat belatedly, as a sign of the decadence of the British aristocracy. But it is generally true that few native English speakers can manage the ' real r-sound ' which is trilled or rolled. This is the vigorous sound /r/ we find in Scottish speech, made by repeatedly and rapidly tapping the tongue-tip against the hard palate or alveolum. It is used by Scots in every possible word-position : ' girl ' = /gɛrɫ/ (/ɛ/ as in /gɛt/ = ' get ') or /gʌrl/ (/ʌ/ as in /bʌt/ = ' but ') ; ' right ' = /rait/ ; ' for ' = /for/, and so on.

Speakers of English south of the border do, in fact, manage an r-sound with a single tap of the tongue on the teeth-ridge when ' r ' comes between two voiced sounds. Listen to the r-sound you make in ' quarrel ' or ' quarry '. It is not fricative ; it has a ghost of the quality of the Scots trilled /r/. We need a special sign for it : /ɾ/.

There is another kind of r-sound which we have to learn if we want to speak French well. This is the '*grasséyé* "r" ' or *uvular* ' r ', made by rolling the uvula against the back of the tongue. It is represented as follows—/R/. We hear this also in Northumberland and Durham : listen to any native singer of the song ' Blaydon Races '. A similar kind of r-sound is produced when there is merely a narrowing of the space between tongue-back and uvula and a uvular fricative ' r ' is produced : /ʁ/.

These ' un-English ' types of r-sound may be listed as follows :

/r/—rolled or trilled ' r '
/ɾ/—one-tap or semi-rolled ' r '
/R/—uvular rolled ' r '
/ʁ/—uvular fricative ' r '

6

Semi-Vowels

A VOWEL-SOUND, as we shall soon see, is made by leaving a space between the tongue and the palate (hard or soft), and then allowing air to pass through the space ; at the same time, of course, the vocal cords are vibrating. But the quality of a vowel-sound is partly determined by what the lips are doing at the same time. For /u/, for instance (the vowel in ' soon ', ' fool ', ' true '), the lips pout, kiss-wise. If we pronounce /u/ vigorously, prolonging the sound, and then suddenly leave off, there will often be an ' after-sound ' produced by the lips themselves—the sound /w/ as in ' well ', ' wit ', ' one '. This is not quite a consonant and not quite a vowel : it is convenient to think of it as a *semi-vowel*. It is a voiced sound, but there is an unvoiced version of it which we represent by ' wh ' in ordinary English spelling—' why ', ' when ', ' what ', ' which '—but by an inverted ' w ' in the IPA : /ʍ/.

We have already seen, in our section on the bilabial fricative, how speakers of foreign languages tend to distrust English /w/ and even consider that it does not exist. Some Welsh speakers have this same notion and give us ' 'oman ' for ' woman ' (this is at least as old as Shakespeare). But English itself has occasionally thrown away its /ʍ/ in words like ' who ' and its derivatives ' whom ' and ' whose ' (/huː/ ; /huːm/ ; /huːz/). It is as though, when the vowel /u/ appears immediately after /ʍ/, the mouth decides that there is no need for mockeries like unvoiced semi-vowels which are a mere ghost of /u/. But the reverse process has taken place with the word ' one ' (/wʌn/). The voiced semi-vowel /w/ seems to be there to remind us that the historically earlier vowel in ' one ' (/o/) was one that required lip-work.

If we pronounce the vowel /i/ (as in ' see ') with great vigour, there is a tendency for the front of the tongue to hit the palate for an instant at the end, producing the ' after-sound ' we hear in its own right as the first sound of ' yes ', ' yet ', ' yoke ', ' yacht '. It seems rather unreasonable to us that the IPA should use /j/ to represent this sound, but it will seem just to the Germans, whose word for ' yes ' is *ja*. Besides, as we shall see, /y/ is needed for another job. This palatal semi-vowel is voiced, but it has an unvoiced companion /ç/—the sound at the beginning of ' huge ', ' humour ', ' Hugh ', and at the end of German *ich, dich, Munich*. It can be thought of as /j/ with /h/ sounding at the same time.

The four semi-vowels can be listed as follows :

/w/—voiced bilabial semi-vowel
/ʍ/—unvoiced bilabial semi-vowel
/j/—voiced palatal semi-vowel
/ç/—unvoiced palatal semi-vowel

7

Palatalisation

WE have completed our survey of the most important consonants and semi-vowels. There are, of course, others—some of them outlandish, some common—which are best considered in other contexts (some of the clicks of African languages, for instance ; a particular semi-vowel in French which requires prior knowledge of the corresponding vowel-sound). Before we move on to the flutes and lutes of speech, leaving the noises behind, we ought to note an interesting phonetic phenomenon which is perhaps less common in English than in the languages of Europe—*palatalisation*. It happens sometimes that a sound associated with, say, the teeth-ridge is, as it were, dragged further into the mouth to be articulated on the hard palate. We have seen how a drunken English-speaker will palatalise ' seat ' to 'sheat ' and ' please ' to ' pleazhe ' (in other words, /s/ becomes /ʃ/ and /z/ becomes /ʒ/). In the Latin languages this palatalisation process works on the nasal /n/ and the lateral consonant /l/. The palatal nasal /ɲ/ sounds to English ears like /nj/, the sound of ' canyon '. French and Italian write it as ' gn ' (*agneau ; agnello*—both meaning ' lamb ') ; Spanish has ' ñ ' (*la uña*— ' the finger-nail ') and Portuguese uses ' nh ' (that Spanish word appears as *a unha*). The palatalisation of /l/ used to exist in French words like *ville* and *fille*, but now only the semi-vowel /j/ quality remains there. But palatalised /l/ continues in Italian (' gl ' as in *megliore*), Spanish (' ll ' as in *llena*), and Portuguese (' lh ' as in *galhina*).

Represented as /ʎ/ in the IPA, it strikes the English ear as an /l/ followed rapidly by /j/—as in 'million' pronounced quickly.

The Russian language is mad about palatalisation. It will palatalise everything, and frequently does. Thus, international words like 'telephone' and 'telegram' appear (I am using the Roman alphabet for greater clarity) as *tyelyefon* and *tyelyegrama*. The word for 'no' strikes some ears as very like a sneer—*nyet*. What will strike the uninstructed, in fact, as a bristle of /j/-sounds is nothing more than the Russian tendency to bring everything to the region of the mouth where /j/ (as in 'yes', remember) is made. The big secret of learning Russian pronunciation lies high in that rocky dome called the hard palate. But more of this later.

FOUR

FLUTES AND LUTES

1

Front Vowels

WE all know what vowels sound like. We must now learn what they
feel like and even *look* like. Sleepless nights can profitably be beguiled
by going through the gamut of English vowels (as in ' Who would
know aught of art must learn, act, and then take his ease ')—silently,
if need be : five-finger exercises on a dummy piano. One finger at least
can be used for checking the tongue-positions and finding out what the
lips are doing ; the first thing that this exploring finger will discover
is that, in the making of vowel-sounds, the tip or point of the tongue is
not used. In practising vowel sounds, the tongue-tip can be tucked
behind the bottom teeth and forgotten. We are concerned with the
front of the tongue (which, at rest, faces the hard palate), the back of
the tongue (which, when lying quietly, faces the soft palate), and the
middle or central bit which lies between front and back. Vowels, of
course, are *voiced* (' vowel ' comes ultimately from the Latin *vocalis*,
which speaks for itself). First we shall find out what vowels can be made
when the front of the tongue is raised towards, or pulled away from,
the hard palate.

Here is a sentence : ' Tea is *thé* in French.' This can be represented
in phonetic script as :

/tiː ɪz te ɪn fɹɛnʃ./

There are, you will note, four vowels : /i/ ; /ɪ/ ; /e/ ; /ɛ/. The vowel /e/
is not found on its own in Queen's English, only in the diphthong /eɪ/
(' way ', ' hay ', ' day '). It is common enough in other languages and
in various English dialects. Let us, for a reason that will be clear very
shortly, concentrate on the three vowels /i/ ; /e/ ; /ɛ/, ignoring /ɪ/ for
the time being. Say /i/ several times and you will discover that the
front of the tongue is raised almost to the limit ; if it were to be raised
any more it would touch the hard palate and the resultant sound

41

would not be a vowel /i/ but the semi-vowel /j/. So /i/ is our high front vowel or *close front vowel* : you cannot have a higher tongue-position, the tongue cannot be closer to the palate without losing the vowel altogether. This is a ' smiling ' vowel : it is the vowel in ' cheese '— word beloved of photographers. The lips are spread.

If now the front of the tongue is lowered a little (and the jaw lowered with it, so that the mouth opens slightly) we get the *half-close front vowel* /e/ (the sound in French *thé*). If the tongue is further lowered (and the jaw with it) we have the vowel in ' French ' or ' men ' or

Fɪɢ. 1.

' debt '—the *half-open front vowel* /ɛ/. Say this trio of vowels over and over again : /i/ ; /e/ ; /ɛ/ ; /i/ ; /e/ ; /ɛ/—ad nauseam. Note the rate of jaw-dropping, tongue-lowering, mouth-opening.

We have three front vowels, then : (1) close ; (2) half-close ; (3) half-open. To complete the sequence, we need a *fully-open* vowel. This will be the a-sound in the French word *café*, the German sound in *Mann*, the Lancashire and Yorkshire vowel in ' man ', ' cat ', ' fat ', ' fan ' and so on. It is *not* the a-sound in the Queen's English pronunciation of those words, though it does appear as the opening sound of the diphthong /aɪ/ in ' fine ', ' wine ', ' die '. /a/, then, is our *open front vowel*.

In pronouncing these four—/i/ ; /e/ ; /ɛ/ ; /a/—take careful note of the way in which the tongue is lowered from the hard palate. The distance between the vowel /i/ and the vowel /e/ is the same as the distance between the vowel /e/ and the vowel /ɛ/. And the tongue travels the same distance from /ɛ/ to /a/ as from /e/ to /ɛ/. When you get up in the morning or, intrigued by your darkling studies, switch the light on and look into a mirror, you will be able to see that the jaw drops, the mouth opens in equal stages. But the movement downwards of the front of the tongue is not precisely vertical : it is oblique and may be presented diagrammatically as in Fig. 1 (page 42).

2

Back Vowels

LET us now try to make a similar sequence of four vowels at the back of the mouth, raising the back of the tongue towards, and then away from, the soft palate. We can start with the vowel /u/—a good clear ' moon-croon-June-tune ' sound made with the tongue well back and the lips rounded as for a kiss (the vowel is, and no wonder, associated with romance). Prolong it, as a child does when it sees the sweet it likes : ' Ooooooooo.' The sound is normally long in English words, appearing as /uː/. Now let us open the lips slightly, allowing the back of the tongue to drop from this high or *close* position to a *half-close* stage. The sound we now get, if the lips remain rounded, is /o/—a pure round o sound which no longer exists in the Queen's English, though French has it in, for instance, *eau, beau, peau.* Pop-singers use the phoneme /o/ consistently, whether they are British or American, when pronouncing words like ' no '. Let the mouth open further, with the lips still round, and the *half-open* position of the tongue gives the sound of ' for ', ' saw ', ' bought ', ' caught ', ' laud ', ' cord '—/ɔ/, normally a long sound (/ɔː/) in English. Finally, if we spread the lips (no more rounding) and utter the sound the doctor asks us to make when he wants to examine our throats, we have the most *open* back vowel of them all—/ɑ/, the sound which appears long (/ɑː/) in English words like ' tar ', ' bar ', ' car ', and so on. Recite the whole sequence many times—/u/ ; /o/ ; /ɔ/ ; /ɑ/—noting the stages of tongue-dropping and mouth-opening. The fall of the back of the tongue is genuinely vertical, so that we may show these vowel-stages in the following way :

FIG. 2.

3

A Vowel Chart

WE have now plotted the tongue-positions for eight vowels—four of them made with the front of the tongue, four of them made with the back of the tongue. We are now in a position to construct a very useful chart, a diagram which represents, in a very square conventional form, the mouth-area in which the tongue operates in order to make vowel-sounds. It is an area guarded by eight vowels which correspond roughly to the cardinal points of a compass ; these vowels are thus called *Cardinal Vowels* (see Fig. 3).

On this chart I have placed certain other vowel-sounds, common in English. /ɪ/ made a brief functional appearance in our sentence ' Tea is *thé* in French '. It is, in fact, the vowel of ' is ', ' in ', ' it ', ' civil ', ' civility ' (in this last word it appears four times). We could not discuss it when dealing with front vowels, for it is not strictly speaking a front vowel at all : the front of the tongue moves in just a little towards the centre of the mouth. Pronounce the word ' easy ' over and over again, and you will be aware of how the front of the tongue moves not merely down but back. Contrast this with the French word *cité* (/site/) and you will feel the difference.

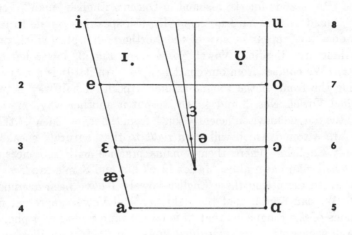

Fɪɢ. 3.

The sound /ʊ/ is the sound you use in ' full ', ' bull ', ' could ', ' wood ', ' stood '. It stands in the same relationship to the back vowels as /ɪ/ to the front vowels: it is advanced a little towards the centre. Lurking in the centre of the diagram (Fig. 3) you will see two spiders, sounds made with the middle of the tongue, both very common in English. /ɜ/ is found long in ' word ', ' bird ', ' sir ', ' fur ' (/wɜːd/; /bɜːd/; /sɜː/; /fɜː/). Like all long vowels in English, it loses some of its length when it appears before an unvoiced consonant, as in ' skirt ', ' shirt ', ' work ', ' earth ' (/skɜ·t/; /ʃɜ·t/; /wɜ·k/; /ɜ·θ/).

There are grounds for supposing that the companion-sound /ə/, which is short, is the commonest sound in English, though the fact that it has no letter in the ordinary alphabet disguises this. It is the ' slack ' sound that comes in the second syllable of ' father ', ' mother ', ' sister ', ' brother ', ' dinner ', ' supper ', and in the first syllable of ' apart ', ' address ' (except in American), ' canoe ', ' conundrum '. It is the indefinite article ' a ' in ' a boy ', ' a girl ', ' a love affair '. It is the tongue at rest in the middle of the mouth, it is colourless and lazy-sounding. The foreigner's clue to the learning of natural-sounding English is found here.

The remaining symbol which I have placed on the chart which is

Fig. 3 is /æ/—a letter we use in ' Caesar ' with the value of /iː/ but which, in the IPA, stands for the a-sound in Queen's English ' man ', ' can ', ' sat ', ' mad '. It is hard for many English-speaking people to learn, as it does not appear in any of the Northern dialects (which prefer something like Cardinal Vowel No. 4 : see Fig. 3, lower left-hand corner). We can see from our chart how to learn it. It is a matter of making the front of the tongue assume a position half-way between Cardinal Vowels Nos. 3 and 4. Or, to put it another way, one must make the tongue move sufficiently south from the /ɛ/ of ' men ', ' then ', ' den ' to a sound which will seem right to the ' natural ' speaker of Queen's English. There then remains practice with sentences like ' That bad man has grabbed Jack's black hat and Sam's cap '.

So far, in discussing these English vowels, I have been evading an issue. We can take it that the eight Cardinal Vowels represent fixed positions of the tongue, so that /i/ is falsely represented as a phoneme if the /i/ we are studying is Cardinal Vowel No. 1. It is an allophone of the /i/-phoneme—|i|—with an unvarying position : the tongue is as high as possible and as far forward as possible. The other three corners of the vowel chart—|a| ; |u| ; |ɑ|—represent similar extreme tongue positions (for |ɑ|, for instance, the mouth is as wide open and the tongue as retracted as possible).

So far so good. But in placing /ɪ/, /ʊ/, /æ/, and the rest in fixed positions on the chart I am committing an absurdity. These cannot have fixed positions : the tongue position of each of them varies from speaker to speaker and, in any individual speaker's set of vowel-sounds, from word to word and from position to position in any given word. Take /ɪ/, for example. It appears five times in the word ' incivility ' (/ɪnsɪvɪlɪtɪ/). Each |ɪ| is subtly different from every other |ɪ|. There are here, in one word, five allophones of the /i/-phoneme. What, in fact, I have done on the vowel chart is to set down certain of my own allophones for these non-cardinal vowels. Your own may be very different.

Here comes a difficult question. At what point does the range of tongue-positions available for, say, the phoneme /i/ meet the range of tongue-positions available for, say, the phoneme /e/ ? If I start right at the very top, with my tongue in the position for Cardinal Vowel No. 1, and then move the tongue imperceptibly down, still producing types of /i/—theoretically an unlimited number of them—I must sooner or later move to a different phonemic area. This, at least, is true in theory. But practice works differently, and we soon find ourselves at the very heart of the phonemic mystery. For to an Englishman ' peat ' (/piˑt/) is manifestly a different word from ' pit ' (/pɪt/)—in other words, /i/ is clearly not the same phoneme as /ɪ/. But to a Frenchman or a Malay it will appear differently : to him /i/ and /ɪ/ will seem to belong to the same family ; in other words, they will sound like allophones and not like phonemes.

It is because it is difficult to ascribe barriers or frontiers to phonemes that so much confusion exists in the world of vowel-sounds. The Northern Englishman, as much as the Chinese, Indian, or French student of English, will be convinced that the Queen's English a-sound in ' man ' is really a form (i.e. an allophone) of the e-sound in ' men '. Foreign students may work for weeks, even months, on minimal pairs (that is, pairs of words in which the difference between the members of the pair is a difference of one sound) and still be unaware of any significant (i.e. phonemic) difference :

leak	lick	dead	dad
seat	sit	said	sad
feet	fit	fed	fad
week	wick	lend	land
greed	grid	pedal	paddle

The recognition of phonemes, the allotment of boundaries to phonemic areas—this is not a mechanical matter but a psychological one. We all carry mental images of vowel-sounds, and these images can persist whatever the tongue is doing. Thus, an Englishman will say /fɪt/, a Frenchman /fit/, and a Scotsman /fet/ or even /fɛt/, but all will hold the same mental image of the word ' fit '. Because of this extreme fluidity of vowels, the lack of physical obstacles to the wandering tongue, languages tend to change. We shall, in a later chapter, see how drastic these changes can be.

4

More Cardinals

Go back to Fig. 3 and recite the eight basic vowels again. You will note that for No. 1 (the sound in ' see ') the lips are spread, for No. 2 (the sound in French *thé*) the lips are spread, and there is the same spreading for No. 3 (the sound in ' men ') and for No. 4 (the sound in the Lancashire pronunciation of ' man '). In other words, these four front vowels are all enunciated with the lips spread—the mouth all set for smiling or grinning and, in the case of No. 4, even for laughing (' hahahahaha '). When we move to No. 5—the back vowel we make for the doctor and pronounce long in ' bar ', ' father ', ' ma '—we find that the mouth is as wide and as square as a letter-box slit : the lip-spreading is extreme. Nos. 1, 2, 3, 4, and 5, then, are vowel-sounds made with the lips spread. Let us digest that.

After digestion, turn to the remaining vowel-sounds which are numbered on the chart : No. 8 (as in ' moon '), No. 7 (as in French *beau* or even the o-sound of English ' obey ' when this word is spoken quickly), No. 6 (as in ' saw '). All of these are pronounced with the lips rounded : for No. 8 they pout ; for No. 7 they express slight surprise ; for No. 6 they show disappointment or pity. Now we must equip ourselves with a conjurer's baton and effect certain remarkable transformations.

Pronounce No. 1 with the lip-rounding of No. 8. It is best to do this by holding on to a long /i/ and then pouting as for /u/. The resultant sound is not an English one, but it will be familiar. It is the sound we hear in the French *lune*, or in the German *Münze*—a *rounded close front vowel* represented in the IPA as /y/.

Pronounce No. 2 with the lip-rounding of No. 7. This is more difficult. The lips should show a pure ' o ', while the tongue holds the /e/ of *thé*, *café* ; this is the sound to be heard in the French *bleu*, *deux*, and in German *hören*, *möglich*. It appears in Danish as ø, and the IPA has borrowed this symbol : /ø/.

Pronounce No. 3 with the lip-rounding of No. 6. This, again, is difficult : it will take some time for the image of the sound to fix itself in the mind. The lips will try to say /ɔ/ in ' saw ' (keep the vowel short) while the tongue is in the position for the /ɛ/ in ' men '. This is represented as /œ/—a symbol derived from French. Indeed, this is the sound you hear in the French words *œuf*, *œuvre*, *neuf*, *heure*. In *un* it is nasalised (/œ̃/).

There is one more piece of lip-rounding to do, and this is not on the remaining front vowel No. 4 (|a|)—a sound which from now is, poor thing, ignored in this context—but on No. 5 (|ɑ|). Here there cannot be any borrowing of lip-rounding from a back vowel, for |ɑ| is itself, of course, a back vowel. What we do is to bring lip-rounding from nowhere, saying a short |ɑ| while our lips form a great circle. This gives us the short vowel in ' not ', ' clod ', ' want ' (in their British pronunciation, that is : the Americans do not use the sound) and a new phonetic symbol |ɒ|.

Having brought over lip-rounding from No. 8 to its opposite number No. 1, and from Nos. 7 and 6 to their respective opposites Nos. 2 and 3, we must practice a little more magic. This time we bring over *lip-spreading* from No. 1 to No. 8, from No. 2 to No. 7, and from No. 3 to No. 6 : we are letting the front vowels work on the back vowels for a change.

If we say No. 8 (|u|) with lips spread (as for No. 1) we get a sound not normally heard in the polite version of any language. It is the ' boo-hoo ' vowel we use when we are crying. Say /u/ as in ' moon ', prolonging the sound ; consciously spread the lips. Ponder on the resultant vowel /ɯ/. You will have heard it used in vulgar speech, where the speaker does not trouble to round his lips for statements like ' You sued him for a new blue suit '. It is not up to us to condemn this vowel. I came near to condemnation, however, when a recent television programme on the Moon used this vowel /ɯ/ consistently. It had the effect of making the moon seem flat and square.

If we say No. 7 (|o|) with the lip-spreading appropriate for No. 2 (|e|) we get a strange vowel represented as |ɤ|. This, again, is not to be found in polite English speech except for the word ' good '. This is normally pronounced /gʊd/, but some speakers drop the vowel to /ɤ/, producing something between ' good ' and ' gud '. A television commercial talks about ' /gɤd/ chocolates '. The vowel, in this context, often seems to have sinister overtones. But it deceives many Southern listeners to Lancashire speech. Lancashire English is commonly supposed to interchange the /ʊ/ of ' put ' with the /ʌ/ of ' butter ', so that ' mother ' is believed to be pronounced /mʊðə/ and ' push ' is believed to be pronounced /pʌʃ/. In actual fact, neither sound is really used at all. Instead, /ɤ/ stands equally for the vowel in ' mother ' and the vowel in ' push '. (Compare this with the bilabial fricative of Sam Weller's speech, discussed in the previous chapter.) It would be profitable to take a sentence and compare the Queen's English (or Southern) and Lancashire pronunciations of the relevant words :

' Don't *rush* upon your *mother*, *utter* threats or even *mutter*,
If she *puts* no *sugar* in your *cup* or on your bread no *butter*.'

Queen's English : /ɪʌʃ/ ; /mʌðə/ ; /ʌtə/ ; /mʌtə/ ; /pʊts/ ; /ʃʊgə/ ; /kʌp/ ; /bʌtə/.

Lancashire English : /ɪʏʃ/ ; /mʏðə/ ; /ʏtə/ ; /mʏtə/ ; /pʏts/ ; /ʃʏgə/ ; /kʏp/ ; /bʏtə/.

The perceptive reader may now guess as to what the next (and last) of these vowels must be. If we pronounce the /ɔ/ of ' awe ', ' caught ', ' lord ' as a short vowel without lip-rounding (in other words, lending the lip-spreading of No. 3 to the tongue-position of No. 6) we have, in fact, this very ' mother ' vowel /ʌ/. Or, rather, we have a cardinal vowel |ʌ| which is an allophone of the total /ʌ/-phoneme. It is a wide phoneme, admitting many variants.

Let us now place these seven new vowels on a chart. Our last chart (Fig. 3) showed the *Primary Cardinal Vowels* ; this new one will show the *Secondary* ones :

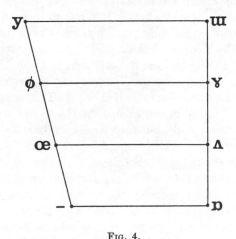

FIG. 4.

Note : We have seen that there are certain semi-vowels which correspond to phonemes we can place on the Primary Cardinal Vowel Chart. Thus, /j/ is a kind of /i/ carried to extremes —the tongue touching the palate instead of merely being close to it—and /w/ is the lip-rounding of /u/ rendered as an audible smack. With one of the Secondary Cardinal Vowels—|y|—we can make a semi-vowel that appears in certain French words. By saying /j/ with the lip-rounding of /y/ we get the semi-vowel /ɥ/—the sound represented by *u* in words like French *muet, huit, lui*.

5

Centralisation

ONE characteristic of very careful English speech—the speech of the trained " elocutionist "—is the tendency to make all front vowels as far front in the mouth as possible and all back vowels as far back as possible—in other words, to emphasise the essential ' frontness ' or ' backness ' of these phonemes. But everyday speech is not so particular : the tongue does not dart forward or push back quite so energetically as in ' trained ' speech, and both front and back vowels approach the middle of the mouth, the central zone where /ɜ/ and /ə/ are made. To represent these centralised vowels we can use the existing phonetic symbols with dots placed over them or a wiggly line (as for ' dark L ') drawn through them. Thus, ' boot ' or ' blue ' pronounced by a Cockney will be made nearer the middle of the mouth than the back, and the pronunciation can be rendered as /büˑt/ or /blü:/. Even with cultivated speakers, forms like ' due ' and ' you ' show centralisation, owing to the influence of the palatal /j/ ; thus we have /djü:/ and /jü:/. A centralised /ɪ/, as in much Australian speech, can be shown as /ï/ or /ɨ/. All these centralised forms are, as far as English is concerned, allophones of the primal front or back phoneme. But the Russian letter ы represents a genuine central phoneme—/ɨ/—in which the tongue tries to say the /ɪ/ of ' sit ', but as far back as possible.

6

Diphthongs

FOR some languages, especially English, a battery of pure vowels—that is, vowels made with a firm and unwavering tongue-position—is not enough. Sometimes the tongue will start at one vowel-position and then move in the direction of another : whether it actually reaches the second vowel-position is not important, for the journey counts more than the arrival.. This sort of tongue-journey gives us the sound known as a *diphthong*, and the phonetic representation shows both the starting-point and the proposed destination. A good example is the personal pronoun ' I ', which is a diphthong starting from /a/ (anywhere in the bottom left-hand corner of the chart in Fig. 3) and moving towards /ɪ/. The phonetic symbol is /aɪ/. Here is a list of English diphthongs :

(*a*) Diphthongs moving towards /ɪ/ :—

/eɪ/—as in ' way ', ' hay ', ' eight '
/aɪ/—as in ' die ', ' high ', ' cry '
/ɔɪ/—as in ' toy ', ' foil ', ' noise '

(*b*) Diphthongs moving towards /ə/ :—

/ɪə/—as in ' ear ', ' beer ', ' mere '
/ɛə/—as in ' air ', ' bare ', ' scarce '
/ɔə/—as in ' oar ', ' hore ', ' coarse '
/ʊə/—as in ' poor ', ' sure ', ' tour '

(*c*) Diphthongs moving towards /ʊ/ :—

/aʊ/—as in ' cow ', ' house ', ' loud '
/oʊ/—as in ' no ', ' know ', ' toe ', ' bone '

(*d*) Triphthongs—the two /a-/ diphthongs followed by /ə/ :—

/aɪə/—as in ' ire ', ' fire ', ' liar '
/aʊə/—as in ' power ', ' flour ', ' shower '

Note that these English diphthongs and triphthongs have as their final element either a fully central sound (/ə/) or a sound approaching the centre—/ɪ/ or /ʊ/. We can make a diphthong chart as in Fig. 5 (the diphthongs on it are, please remember, the ones I myself make). A vast number of variants is possible. For instance, we hear /eɪ/ as /ɛɪ/ or even /æɪ/ in quite cultivated speech, while /oʊ/ can be anything from /ɣʊ/ to /əʊ/. In learning foreign languages we may try to impose our own diphthongal habits on a very different sound-system, but we can avoid this if we remember that English is nearly unique in posses-sing the central and near-central vowels which form the second elements of our diphthongs. Moreover, what sound like diphthongs in such languages as Italian are more often two vowels, fully enunciated, following each other rapidly, as in /ai/. And the German diphthongs of

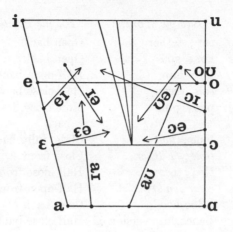

Fig. 5.

klein (/klain/) and *Haus* (/haus/) tend to reach (or very nearly) a second element which is fully forward (/i/) or fully back (/u/). The English language dearly loves the middle of the mouth.

We are now in a position to make a fairly comprehensive list of vowel-sounds :—

Phonetic Symbol	Sample Word(s)	Tongue Position	State of Lips
(a) /i/	sea ; *si*	Close front	Spread
/ɪ/	sit ; will	Less close, less front	Spread
/e/	*thé ; café*	Half-close, fully front	Spread
/ɛ/	men ; *père*	Half-open, fully front	Spread
/æ/	man ; cat	More open, fully front	Spread
/a/	man ; cat (Lancs.)	Fully open, fully front	Spread
/ɜ/	word ; girl	Central	Spread
/ə/	the ; ' a ' in allow	Central	Spread

Phonetic Symbol	Sample Word(s)	Tongue Position	State of Lips
/ɑ/	car ; father	Open back	Spread
/ɒ/	not ; god	Open back	Rounded
/ɔ/	for ; law	Half-open back	Rounded
/o/	*eau ; beau*	Half-close back	Rounded
/ʊ/	put ; pull	More close, less back	Rounded
/u/	blue ; *tout*	Close, fully back	Rounded
(b) /y/	*lune ; Führer*	Close front	Rounded
/ø/	*bleu ; böse*	Half-close front	Rounded
/œ/	*cœur ; œuf*	Half-open front	Rounded
/ɯ/	' Boo-hoo '	Close back	Spread
/ɤ/	Lancashire version of ' u ' in ' but '	Half-close back	Spread
/ʌ/	mother ; but (Queen's English)	Half-open, back or slightly centralised	Spread

FIVE

SOUNDS IN ACTION

1

So far we have been discussing the sounds of language in a void, dissecting and probing as on some cold pathologist's slab. To talk of /p/ or /b/ or /i/ or /u/ is to talk of an abstraction—something taken out of the warm current of speech. Now we must put the sounds back in again and see how they behave in company with other sounds. We want to examine, not bare phonemes, but words, phrases, babble and gabble.

We have already referred, in passing, to that attribute of vowel-sounds which is called *length*. Some phonemes take longer to say than others : /si:d/ takes about twice as long as /si·t/ ; /si·t/ takes about twice as long as /sɪt/. Length of vowel varies from dialect to dialect in English. An Englishman will, for instance, accept /mæn/ as the normal native pronunciation of ' man ' ; he will regard /mæːn/ as ' trans-atlantic '. And indeed there is an American tendency to ' drawl ' or lengthen vowels which is in marked contrast to the so-called ' clipped ' British habit. But even within the limits of an *idiolect*—one person's mode of speech—there will be shortenings or lengthenings of vowel-sounds according to context. For instance, if I say ' Give it to her '— stressing the ' Give ', as though the person addressed is holding the thing back—the vowel of ' her ' will be short (/ɜ/). If now I stress the ' her ' (' Give it to *her*, not to him '), the vowel will take on full length (/ɜː/). And so, in ' Where has she *been* ? ', the /i/ of ' been ' appears long (/iː/). In ' She's been to *London* ', /i/ is quite short. ' I asked you what you heard, not what you saw ' gives us the last word with a fully long /ɔː/. ' I saw nothing at all of the film ' has a ' saw ' with a quite short /ɔ/.

Still, we tend to think of certain vowels in English as *naturally* long : /iː/ as in ' see ' ; /uː/ as in ' you ' ; /ɔː/ as in ' paw ' ; /ɑː/ as in ' far '. We think of a shortening of these as a kind of perversion of their essential quality, just as we regard a lengthening of /æ/ to /æː/ or /ɪ/ to

/ɪː/ as a deformation of those sounds. And so, with the notion of a *long* vowel in our mental ears, we have difficulty in mastering the short /i/ and /u/ of languages like Spanish. Italian lengthens vowels before double consonants, so that *bello* sounds like *beeeeello* to some ears. We have to learn when to lengthen and when to keep short.

Length is allophonic, not phonemic : ' seed ' can be pronounced as /siːd/ or as /sid/ and still be recognisably the same word. But an Englishman hearing a Frenchman pronounce ' peace ' as /pis/ instead of /piˑs/ may be unsure what vowel the Frenchman *intends*—whether /ɪ/ (which will transform a word of noble connotations to a rough lavatory one) or the right phoneme /iː/. Length is a vowel-attribute to be carefully watched.

Another important attribute in languages of Germanic origin— English, Dutch, German, Danish, Swedish, Norwegian—is that known as *stress*. It is also vital in Slavonic tongues like Russian, but it has little to do with the Romance languages—French, Italian, Spanish, and the rest. Every English word has—if it possess more than one syllable—its own characteristic stress, and stress (indicated by the sign /'/ before the syllable concerned) can sometimes determine meaning, besides affecting the quality of the phonemes which make up the word. Thus, ' increase ' as /'ɪnkriˑs/ is a noun denoting ' addition or enlargement ', whereas ' increase ' as /ɪn'kriˑs/ is a verb meaning ' to enlarge, to add to '. ' Compact ' can appear as /kəm'pækt/—an adjective meaning ' firmly united or joined together ' ; it can also be /'kɒmpækt/—a noun with various meanings, one of which is ' a lady's portable vanity-box '. So also ' conduct ' is a verb as /kən'dʌkt/ and a noun as /'kɒndʌkt/.

This lexical differentiation, as we may call it, makes the stress of a number of English words very important, but the shifting of stress may—without actually altering meaning—bring about profound phonemic changes. The ' correct ' pronunciation of ' controversy ' has the stress on the first syllable, while a pronunciation that has gained wide currency (and hence cannot really be judged ' wrong ') has the stress on the second syllable. Compare the two : (1) /'kɒntrəvɜˑsɪ/ ; (2) /kən'trɒvəsɪ/. The two vowel-sequences are quite different. So are they in ' purport ' as a noun—/'pɜˑpət/—and ' purport ' as a verb— /pə'pɔˑt/.

Stress is heavy in English words and heavier still in Russian, nor, in either language, does ordinary spelling give any indication as to where emphasis should be thrown. That is why it is a relief to go back to the unemphatic flow of French after tussling with the capricious hammer-strokes of the language of Dostoevsky and Mr Khrushchev. Stress means little in French and little in Italian ; the mild stresses of Spanish are always regular and so take care of themselves : in fact, the daughters of Latin are not at all as one would expect—tempestuous and fist-banging. Greek, whose only daughter is modern Greek, was no more concerned about stress than Latin seems to have been—not, anyway, to judge from the stress-variability of the following Greek derivatives in English :

photograph—/ˈfoʊtəgrɑ·f/ (or -/græf/)
photographic—/ˈfoʊtəˈgræfɪk/
photographer—/fəˈtɒgrəfə/

Stress has an important part to play in those meaningful groups of words we call sentences or phrases. We have to use a new set of signs to show emphatic syllables and weak syllables here—a kind of Morse (dash for stress ; dot for no-stress) :

Where do you think you're going ?

But as soon as we start considering the rhythms of whole statements we are inevitably led to that other attribute of speech—intonation, speech-melody, the rise and fall of the voice. This is a huge subject we can only touch on briefly here. Certainly, the tunes of English are subtly important, conveying not only meaning but social attitudes. Take the following, for example :

I expect you'll want a wash   I expect you'll want a wash

The first seems inoffensive enough—an offer of ablution facilities to a guest who has just arrived off a long journey. The second implies several things : the speaker is not very willing to give anything (even water, soap, and the use of a towel) ; yet at the same time there is a faint suggestion that the person addressed is habitually dirty, not just travel-stained.

c

On the level of pure lexical meaning, intonation can turn a statement into a question :

He's going now

He's going now ?

The intonation patterns of other languages can be learned by listening : foreign radio stations supply as much as one needs for an elementary image. At least, this is so with European languages. When one comes to a *tonal* language like Chinese one faces very large difficulties indeed. What we may call (though the time has not yet come to define the term accurately) the *words* of Chinese are all formed in the same way : they are monosyllables, either closed (consonant at the end) or open (vowel at the end). Thus, the sentence ' A teapot is used for making tea and a kettle for boiling water ' is rendered as :

Ch'a hu shih p'ao ch'a yung ti, shui hu shih shao shui yung ti.

(This is in the national Chinese dialect known as *Kuo-yü*.) If you consider the limited number of phonemes that are available to the human mouth, you will see that there are not enough different monosyllables available to make all the words that a complex civilisation needs in its language. Consider how we would fare if English were made up solely of monosyllables, if all sentences were like ' My friend John says that it is high time you went to the Bank to get some cash to pay him what you owe him '. Already we have a fair number of monosyllables which have the same sound but different meanings—like ' know '/' no ' ; ' way '/' weigh ' ; ' I '/' aye '/' eye '. Consider how many of these *homophones*, as they are called, there must be in Chinese. The following sentence—*Ma ma ma ma*—can mean ' Mother has scolded the horse '. This is no joke.

In order, then, to differentiate between monosyllables made up of the same sounds but carrying different meanings, Chinese makes use of *tones*. In *Kuo-yü* (the National Language) there are five, though the fifth is falling into disuse. These are :

1. *Shang P'ing Shêng*—a sharp falling tone.
2. *Hsia P'ing Shêng*—a curt upper rising tone.
3. *Shang Shêng*—a long rising tone ' broken in the middle '.

4. *Ch'ü Shêng*—a ' departing tone '—a falling-away melody.

5. *Ju Shêng*—an abrupt intonation which shortens the vowel.

In learning a sentence like *Mên k'ou yu jên* (' There is someone at the door ') we have to learn the tone which helps give each word its meaning, thus : *Mên* 2 ; *k'ou* 3 ; *yu* 3 ; *jên* 2. The difficulties involved in tackling a tonal language are great but not insuperable. No language is all that difficult if we learn to understand its idiosyncracies. Chinese is fascinating.

2

A POINT I made above is that it is possible to learn the intonations and stress-system of a language by listening—so long as one listens long enough and attentively enough. But it is not so easy to learn the phonemes of a foreign language by listening—despite the claims of certain gramophone record companies. Children, if they are young enough, can pick up foreign sounds accurately : it is instructive, in Malaya, to listen to the perfect mastery of Chinese tones evinced by British children with Chinese amahs. Rare mimics—and all mimics are rare—can grasp a foreign sound-system almost instinctively : one thinks of Peter Sellers in England, Danny Kaye in America. But the great majority of language-learning adults cannot imitate sounds with any approach to exactness : told to try /y/ in French *lune*, they will say something like /i/ or something like /u/, but never the compromise sound that is the right one. To ask most adults to imitate the sounds they hear is like asking a non-pianist to listen to a Bach fugue on the radio and then sit down at the keyboard and rattle the music off. Only a knowledge of phonetics can show us the way through foreign mysteries.

I must emphasise that by ' a knowledge of phonetics ' I do not mean merely a knowledge of the *International Phonetic Alphabet*. The symbols, despite what many teachers seem to think, have no validity in themselves : they are merely signals relating to actions of the vocal organs. But, if I have put in some time on tongue-raising and lip-spreading, I will know what exactly the symbol /i/ can mean when I meet it in a dictionary. It is important, incidentally, that any foreign-language dictionary we buy should be big enough and scholarly enough to give pronunciation in the symbols of the IPA. It is a waste of money to buy some match-box sized amateurish lexicon which gives 'approximate' pronunciations in a variant of ordinary English orthography—like *kaffay* for *café*, or *bam-bee-noh* for *bambino*. The French–English dictionary I possess cost rather more than a bottle of gin, but it is worth spending money on a professional performance. I look up the word *homme* and find, before the definition, the phonetic rendering /ɔm/. I know that the first of these two symbols stands for a *short* sound in the region of Cardinal Vowel No. 6 (Fig. 3). If I take something like the /ɔ/ in ' fought ' (/fɔ·t/), only very much shortened, so that it takes almost no time to utter, I am in the correct phonemic area. /m/ causes no difficulty. I want to say, not just *homme* (' man '), but ' a man '—*un homme*. I look up *un* and find /œ̃/. Here I have a phoneme in the region of Secondary Cardinal Vowel No. 3. I revise the technique for saying it—a form of /ɛ/ with the lip-rounding appropriate to /ɔ/, snorted through the nose—and I practise saying it.

But learning to pronounce *un homme* correctly is not just a matter of getting two words right : add one word to another word, and the answer is not two words—it is a new entity, a phrase. So now I have to note that, though the dictionary gives *un* as /œ̃/, something special happens when *un* appears before a vowel—in this case, the /ɔ/ of *homme*. The *n* of *un*—normally silent—acts as a link between the two vowels (/œ̃/ and /ɔ/) and is pronounced. /œ̃/ + /ɔm/ = /œ̃nɔm/.

The problems that English speakers of French encounter when trying to differentiate between *femme* (' woman ') and *faim* (' hunger ') are overcome if a little phonetic thought is taken. The dictionary gives the following pronunciations : *Faim*—/fɛ̃/ ; *femme*—/fam/. The second word is straightforward : the /f/ and /m/ are found in the English sound-system as well as the French ; the /a/ is lower than the /æ/ in ' man ', the jaw drops more for it. As for /fɛ̃/—we know that /ɛ/ is somewhere near Cardinal Vowel No. 3 (Fig. 3) and that it is nasalised, snorted through the nostrils. To fix the difference between the two words we must now practise a whole phrase—*La femme a faim* (' The woman is hungry ') : /la fam a fɛ̃/. The difficulty of distinguishing between the pronunciations of the two words can be overcome in a very short time. Phonetics is the key.

If we can use phonetics for breaking down foreign words in this manner, we ought also to use our knowledge of how sounds are made, and how sounds can be scientifically notated, to study the allophonic differences within the English language—what for example makes an Australian pronunciation of ' No ' different from that of an American or Queen's English version of it. Experiment is required : the tongue has to travel about, searching, and the ear keep on the alert. The diphthong /ou/ (in ' no ', ' go ') is very variable as far as the first element /o/ is concerned, but the second element usually remains pretty stable. Thus, British English is capable of /ɜʊ/, /əʊ/, even (though this is extreme) /eʊ/ : what gives the diphthong its ' oh ' character is the second element—the tongue reaching towards /ʊ/. But it seems certain that no user of a diphthong in words like ' show ', ' though ' allows the first element to drop as low as, say, the /ɑ/ of ' car ' (pronounced short) or the /a/ of French *café*. To do so would be to risk producing a diphthong proper only to words like ' now ', ' house '—a sort of /aʊ/. This limits the area in which the tongue can search for a first element in Australian ' no '. Try /ɜʊ/ ; try /əʊ/ ; try /øʊ/, even. It is clear that none of these will do—they are altogether too ' Pommie ' or U.K. English. The untutored ear fancies that Australian ' no ' is something like ' now '. But /aʊ/, as we have seen, is not an accurate rendering. Move the back of the tongue higher ; try /ʌʊ/. That seems more like it—a diphthong starting off with the vowel of ' up '. Try /ɤʊ/ : that seems *very* much more like it.

How about American ' no ? ' Experiments will probably end up with something like /ou/. How about the ' no ' of Welshmen ? Listen carefully. There seems to be no second element there ; the sound does not seem to be a diphthong at all. It is a half-open vowel, not far from Cardinal Vowel No. 6 (Fig. 3)—something like a very round /ɔ/.

Dialectology is the name we give to the study of the make-up of the regional variants of a language. To travel England with the Cardinal Vowel Charts clear in one's head, a notebook and pencil handy—this can be fascinating. It is more than a mere amusing hobby, however : it is vital, a fingering of the warm pulse of human language.

SIX

SOUNDS IN SPACE

An alphabet seems the most natural thing in the world to people brought up on ABC bricks, but—if this were not a sober book—I should be betrayed into large enthusiasms about the 'miracle' of its invention, placing it high above television, jet propulsion, and nuclear fission. It is clever enough to be able to record and reproduce by electronic means the sounds our mouths utter, but the conversion of speech into impulses and impulses into speech cannot match the fundamental achievement of converting the temporal into the spatial—for speech works in time, but letters stand in space.

It is doubtful if the Alphabet is much more than 3,000 years old, whereas speech is nearly as old as man. Thus, the dawning of the principle of representing a spoken sound by a written letter has come very late in our history, and it still has not come to a large proportion of mankind—the Chinese, for example. The Alphabet is the last and most efficient device for giving symbolic permanence to the spoken word. Unlike fire and agriculture, it did not come at various times to various races—widely separated in space but undergoing parallel developments. It came once and once only to a race of Semites trading in the Mediterranean lands, and—like many epoch-making discoveries—it came almost in a fit of absent-mindedness.

Before the Alphabet, there were certain rough and cumbersome ways of giving permanence to words, but these had nothing to do with words as temporal events, successions of speech-sounds. The Egyptians, the Mexicans, the Red Indians drew pictures which stood for words—they got behind the word itself and recorded what the word stood for. Picture-writing is our oldest form of setting down signs for the *referents* of language (that is, the things in the outside world that language refers to), and it has always been the least efficient.

The reason for this is, of course, that there are comparatively few aspects of language that lend themselves to adequate pictorialisation. We can draw the sun, the moon, spears, jugs, loaves, stylised men, and horses, but a statement even of so simple a type as ' I lost my wife and five children in the last inter-village war ' is hard to set down in pure pictures. The fact is that the *pictograms* (to use the technical term) of the pre-alphabetic civilisations were never really intended to provide a comprehensive writing system : we tend to impose our own needs on societies quite happy without mail-boxes, libraries, and daily news-papers. Pictograms probably only arose as reminders, signs of owner-ship, commemorative inscriptions. Consider how little urge there would be to make inscriptions at all when there were only stones and chisels as writing implements : if we had to leave the smooth ease of pen-and-ink and typewriter to go back to painful hammering, writing would die out quickly enough.

But the pictogram still retains its usefulness, even in our sophisticated alphabetic societies. It is the most primitive and naïve of all inscriptive techniques, but it can prevent—in international youth hostels—a male from using a female bathroom, and vice versa : the conventional symbol for a male is a two-legged stick-man, that for a female the same, only with a skirt. Zig-zagging lines will represent running water ; a bed will show a dormitory. Our traffic signs show a fair variety of picto-grams : a cross for a cross-roads, a zed for a bend, a T for a road junc-tion, a schoolboy and schoolgirl for a school (this pictogram used to be an *ideogram* or *logogram*—terms we shall come to in a moment. There was a symbolic torch representing the *idea* of learning ; this may have been too complex for many drivers, hence the reversion to a primitive pictogram).

The development of writing is associated with a number of different social functions which, on close examination, are seen to be cognate. The growth of agriculture involves star-gazing and moon-watching—in other words, attempts to establish the limits of the seasons. Also, fertility rituals are performed and gods of fertility are worshipped. A priestly class emerges—elders who have no other work than to perform due ceremonies, predict drought or abundance, intercede with the gods. It is difficult, in these early societies, to separate religion from agriculture : the priest is a magician is an astrologer is an astronomer is a scientist. He guards sacred mysteries ; he needs to keep complex records ; he compiles the tables of the law. By now simple pictograms are by no means enough : we are in the age of secret sophisticated writings, sacred carvings or *hieroglyphics*.

FIG. 6.—Some Chinese Characters.

We are, in fact, in priest-ruled Egypt, with its holy men who learn how to predict the rise and fall of the Nile but are inevitably unwilling to share their secrets with others. Their kind of writing seems to use straightforward pictograms—which, theoretically, any plain man can understand, just as any plain motorist can understand traffic signs— but in reality they use a priestly code, communication between the elect, holy and terrible symbols. An Egyptian priest would be a fool to make his system of writing common knowledge ; he plays up the mystery of language and enhances his own power ; he has a vested interest in codes and acrostics and other means of delimiting a system of communication to a chosen few.

There were various means of creating inscriptive symbols which should transcend the limitations of pictograms. One way was the way of metaphor. The Chinese to this day use a drawing of a man or a field to represent respectively these two words, bringing the symbols together to make the new word ' farmer '. That is easy enough, but how about abstract words, words like, for instance, ' not ' ? ' Not ' in Chinese shows a sort of plant with a line above it : the plant is trying to grow, but the line seems to be stopping it. This is a little poem of negativeness, a metaphor of ' notness '. The Chinese word for ' bright ' brings together two symbols—that for the sun and that for the moon : two concrete images suggest a common property, abstracted into the word ' brightness '. That is another way of doing it.

When, in fact, symbols are used to express ideas rather than to represent objects in the external world, we have *ideograms* (' idea drawings ') or *logograms* (' word drawings '). With some of these (Chinese ' not ' is a good example) it is possible to see vestiges of picture-writing ; with many the pictorial origins are obscure and the shapes seem quite arbitrary. Thus, the Arabic numerals seem (except for the first) to relate to nothing pictorial : 2, 3, 4, 5, and the rest are arbitrary characters which have no universal verbal significance (1 is *un* to the French, *ein* to the Germans, *satu* to the Malays) but in all countries carry the same arithmetical meaning. They are true ideograms. The Roman numerals come closer to pictograms, especially when they appear on a clock-face—I, II, III, IIII, V. They are drawings of fingers, except for V which represents the space between index finger and thumb and thus stands for the whole hand. Signs like +, =, % have clear meanings to everyone, but they do neither a pictorial

o*

nor a phonetic job (' + ' does not show the sounds of ' plus ') ; they are pure ideograms.

The modern Chinese language contrives to get on very well with its ideograms : it produces books on Marxism and nuclear physics ; the bulk of the literate are not noticeably clamouring for a Western alphabet. But, occasionally, especially when introducing a foreign word, Chinese becomes suddenly aware of sounds and forgets all about referents : it will transliterate a foreign name like Churchill not by using the ideograms for a church and a hill but by choosing words which carry roughly the same sounds as the English name. This puzzles some readers of Chinese newspapers, for pronunciation varies so widely all over China that it is not possible for the ideograms chosen to convey the same sounds to everybody. I was once in the company of two Chinese who could not understand each other's dialect. They were able to converse only by writing down their words as ideograms. The parallel of monoglot Englishmen and Russians finding common ground in symbols like 159% is an exact one.

As soon as sound-elements are introduced into non-alphabetic writing, as soon as a symbol represents a phonetic rather than a semantic notion, then we are on the way to learning our ABC. The first glimmerings of phonetic writing among the Egyptian priests appear in puns, play on words with the same sound but with different meanings : homophones, in fact. It is easiest to understand this sort of trick if we think of the possibilities of English homophones. Let us imagine that we are in the same position as the Egyptian priests, possessing no alphabet, only pictograms. We have the word ' sun ', and ' sun ' is easy enough to represent : all that is required is a circle with a few wiggly lines for rays. We also have the word ' son ', and ' son ' is not so easy to draw : we can, after much trouble, achieve a fair likeness of a young man, but how can we denote relationship ? The easiest thing to do is to use our pictogram for ' sun ' for ' son ', exploiting the homophonic. This will normally be enough, for context should make all clear : ' The father loves his /sʌn/ ' is not ambiguous. But, to avoid confusion in statements like ' The /sʌn/ sank into the sea ', it might be useful to prefix the ' sun ' pictogram with a conventional sign denoting human maleness. The image of a man would do. Let us take another example : ' sea ' and ' see '. ' Sea ' is easily shown as wavy water ; if we want the verb ' to see ' we can put the image of a human eye in front of it ; if we want 'see' in its episcopal sense, how about a simple drawing of a chess-bishop? This way of defining by means of prefixes will give us a whole set of little signs called *radicals*. The eye-radical followed by the drawing of a watch will indicate clearly what verb is meant; the man-radical can give the pictogram of a buoy a completely unambiguous meaning. Radicals exist in Chinese, and the learning of them eases recognition of certain words. When a radical is fused with a pictogram and, over long years, simplified and conventionalised, it becomes difficult to pick out the representational element from the resultant ideogram.

This kind of punning—which, incidentally, must often have been deliberately formed to confuse rather than enlighten—is still very popular in children's-page competitions. The most elaborate type of pun is the multiple or syllabic—'horsefly' shown as a horse and a fly; 'well-bred' as a well and a loaf; a chair, a man, and a ship to make up 'chairmanship'. One can go to excruciating lengths—as in charades—with 'Socratic' (a sock, a rat, a 'this-sum-is-right' ideogram) or—which deforms the word somewhat, but no matter—a paper-clip, a toe, a horse's mane and an ear for 'kleptomania'. These tricks and puzzles fossilise a stage of emergence towards the syllabic sense: one more step and we shall have an alphabet.

Everybody is able to recognise a syllable, even if some difficulty is experienced in defining what a syllable is. The old notion that a syllable was a vowel or a combination of vowel and one or more consonants will not really do. In a word like 'rhythm' there are recognisably two syllables, but the second of them need not have a vowel: /rɪðm̩/. In fact, we use the symbol of a vertical line under a consonant symbol to indicate that that consonant is syllabic. Here are other examples: 'fission'—/fɪʃn̩/; 'nation'—/neɪʃn̩/; 'national'—/næʃn̩l̩/. If we think of a syllable as a sound or group of sounds pronounced in a single impulse, we have a tentative definition that is unsatisfactory but, for the moment, will serve. Everybody can, then, recognise a syllable and can accurately count the number of syllables in a given word, but not many can give the number of *sounds*. 'Civility' has four syllables: everybody will recognise that. The number of sounds will be guessed at from the number of letters and, for once, the guess will be right. But how many sounds are there in the disyllables 'open'; 'fair-ground'; 'butcher'? How many in the trisyllables 'possible';

' photograph ' ; ' pertinent ' ; ' Westminster ' ? To the person with the minimum of phonological training there should be no difficulty in giving the right answer ; to the majority there will come an accession of head-scratching and doubt.

It is no wonder, then, that with the men of a few thousand years ago there should be no urge to dissect words into phonemic units. Syllables, however, were a different matter, and the first breakthrough from a priestly script (hieroglyphics) to a demotic or popular one was easy and natural enough : the old pictograms, in a conventionalised and simplified form, were turned into the materials of *syllabaries*. A syllabary thinks in terms of a single symbol standing for a consonant plus a vowel. It works best with languages like Japanese, where every word can be broken up into syllables each following that easy formula : YO-KO-HA-MA ; HI-RO-SHI-MA ; MI-KA-DO.

Not that Japanese makes exclusive use of a syllabary. It is a language which early adopted the ideograms of Chinese but finds a syllabary useful when new or foreign words have to be presented. Chinese does not like borrowing from other languages ; it prefers to re-formulate a new idea in its own terms, so that ' electricity ' is rendered as ' light spirit ' and ' gas ' as ' coal spirit '. But Japanese will gladly accept English words like ' gas ', ' page ', ' bus '. ' pound ', ' dress ', and ' typewriter ', so long as it can fit them to the native sound-pattern as *gazu, peju, basu, pondo, doresu*, and *tuparaita* respectively. To get these words on to paper it will use a syllabary—either the *Hiragana* or the *Katakana*. In fact, written and printed Japanese makes use of both of these, together with about 1,500 Chinese ideograms.

The *Katakana* syllabary has five symbols corresponding to the five vowel-letters A I U E O. It then has five corresponding to the syllables MA MI MU ME MO, five corresponding to NA NI NU NE NO, five corresponding to SA SI SU SE SO, and so on—the remaining consonants Z P B T D K G Y R H W each possessing five forms according to the vowel—A I U E or O—which is attached to it. This gives 14 × 5 = 70 symbols + 5 (vowels on their own) + the solitary closed form (i.e. ending in a consonant) UN = 76. This is about the average number of signs required for a syllabary. Fig. 7 shows an article I wrote for a syndicate of Japanese newspapers (the subject is Russia). In it you will notice the whole consort dancing together—Chinese ideograms, *Hiragana*, and *Katakana* syllabaries. My own name appears to the

英作家のみたソ連の民衆生活

アンソニー・バージェス

のんびり

【本社特約OCS通信】英国の小説家アンソニー・バージェス氏はこのほどソ連のレニングラードを訪問し、帰英後BBC放送で旅行談を放送した。次に紹介するのはそのときの放送談話大要であるが、いわゆるソ連国民の非能率ぶりとか一般舌についても作家らしい機知に富んだ解釈を示し多くの示唆をふくんだ観察を行なっている。

"能率"は上層部だけのもの?

私はソ連人の能率の悪い点が一番好きである。鉄のように冷たく厳しい社会生活を予想して、私はレニングラードを訪れたのだが、そこで見たのは最もヒューマンな人間、べつのことばでいえば最も非能率的な人間であった。

といっても非能率的な国民がスプートニクや宇宙飛行士を生み出すはずはないのだが、おそらく能率というものはソ連社会では一番の上層部に浮いている薄いエキスのようなものなのだろう。学校にたとえてみると先生方はみな職員会議に集まっているか最高学級の物理実験に立ち合い、生徒たちは教室で自習をしているようなものは間違いで、ソ連人が

る。また英字新聞の賣れおら、英国共産党のデイリ……カー紙しかおいていない……開売子の少女は「ほかの新聞はもう売り切れ」し……う。

もしかしたらこれを、ワのは間違いで、ソ連人が

Fig. 7.

right—just left from the title in its hatched or shaded box. It is read from top to bottom as A-UN-SO-NI BA-ZI-YE-SU, which is, to Japanese ears, near enough to *Anthony Burgess*.

In the East, then, one may see all the pre-alphabetic sign-systems in daily use : the pictogram, the ideogram, and the syllabary. There, however, there has been no sense of the need to take that extra step towards a true alphabet. Admittedly, it is a difficult extra step, and it was only achieved by the Semitic peoples of the Mediterranean because of an accident—that accident being the peculiar structure of Semitic languages.

All Semitic languages—Hebrew, Arabic, Phoenician, and the rest—possess in common a peculiar devotion to consonants. In fact, a Semite does not think of a Semitic word as being made of syllables (consonant plus vowel) ; he thinks of it as being made of the strong bones of consonants with the vowel sounds floating above like invisible spirits. Moreover, the vowels of a Hebrew or Arabic word have little to do with the determination of meaning : meaning is firmly staked out by the consonants alone. Thus, the three consonants K-T-B in Arabic possess a root meaning of ' reading ', so that *kitab* means ' book ', *khatib* means ' mosque reader ', the prefix ' m- ' makes *maktaba*—' bookshop ' or *mokhtab*—' college '. The consonants alone will establish meaning if the context is clear. In Hebrew the staking-out of three consonants to create a word gives a characteristic flavour to proper names like Jacob, Rachel, David, Moloch, and Joseph. Spell the words as JCB, RCHL, DVD, MLCH, JSPH and the meanings remain clear—in Hebrew. English is a language which defines meaning as much with vowels as with consonants, and so DVD is too ambiguous as it stands : it could be, besides ' David ', ' divide ' or ' dived '. And MLCH could be, besides ' Moloch ', ' milch ', or ' mulch '. Only in the Semitic languages—rich in consonants but comparatively poor in vowels—can a group of consonants stand for the whole word.

We believe that the Phoenician traders of the Mediterranean were the first to take over simplified Egyptian symbols and use these to represent consonants. They created a *betagam* instead of an *alphabet* : a BCD, not an ABC. They were not interested in finding vowel-letters, because vowel-letters were not necessary in the writing of Phoenician—a Semitic language. This meant that they were able to make do with twenty-odd symbols—a tremendous and epoch-making economy. Had they thought—as speakers of non-Semitic languages like English and Japanese must think—in terms of consonant-plus-vowel, they would not have been able to leap beyond a syllabary of seventy-odd symbols, for Mediterranean man was not yet ready for the concept of vowels and consonants as independent partners in language. But the Phoenicians

FIG. 8.—Origin and Development of A, M, O, R.

had the concept of *free consonants*, and this made their discovery of a betagam or BCD possible.

What urged them to create this system of easily learned and handled letters ? Not literature, not religion, but trade. They presumably needed to make out their bills and enter their books with some speed . a few quick strokes, and there was a memo or a delivery note or an invoice. Not for them the leisure of hieroglyphics or syllabaries. An

Egyptian eye or head, bird or running water must become mere abstract lines or circles—as with the letters of our own alphabet, which ultimately have the same derivation. Whether their letters would be curved or angular must depend on the materials used : our own A and T and K are essentially *chiselled* letters ; the curved forms like S and O and U suggest a softer ground, like paper, and the squiggling motions of a reed-pen (see Fig. 8).

In which direction did their letters travel—left to right, right to left, up, down ? It varied ; it did not seem to be of much consequence. Our

H{V H J
 {W

JHVH = Jehovah

D V D

DVD = David

M H R B A

ABRHM = Abraham

L BH B

BBHL = Babyl(on)

L ' {V M S
 {W

Samuel

Fig. 9.—Some Biblical names in Hebrew script unpointed (i.e. without indication of vowel-sounds). The letter *Aleph* is represented here as meaning either ' A ' or ' ' '. Actually it has no equivalent in English : it is a ' smooth breathing '— not a vowel at all. In both Hebrew and Arabic script we must read from right to left.

own left–right habit is not based on any law of nature, any more than traffic rules are. When it comes to painting a name on a factory chimney, we are as ready as are the Chinese or Japanese to start at the top and move down. The two great Semitic languages have settled for opening a book at the back and reading from right to left (see Figs. 9 and 10).

When I first learned to use Arabic script I feared I would get ink on my sleeve : it soon seemed to me the most natural and the cleanest—as well as the most sensuously satisfying—way of writing imaginable.

The earliest Semitic scripts have survived only fragmentarily, leaving no literature or tables of the law. The Hebrew and Arabic alphabets are very much with us to-day. The examples given in Figs. 9 and 10 show how important the consonantal letters are. Hebrew script has kept itself strictly to the Hebrew peoples and those few non-Semites who have been Judaised ; Arabic script has travelled the world with the Arab traders and missionaries and been imposed on alien races along with Islam ; wherever the flag of the star and crescent has been planted, the Arabic alphabet has been planted too—from the Indus to Spain and furthest east of all to the Indies. This has led to various modifications of the alphabet to fit the non-Semitic structure of languages like Spanish and Malay. Malay, for instance, is allowed to use more vowel-signs than would be thought proper in Mecca, though even then it keeps them down to a minimum. Persian (and this comes as a surprise to many) is an Aryan language, belonging to the same family as English and French and Russian, and it has not really taken kindly to the imposition of an alphabet that is nearly all consonants. If the Arabs had conquered England in the Middle Ages (and this might well have happened), English would have had to fit itself into the straitjacket of the Islamic BCD. How some English names take to this treatment is shown in Fig. 10.

So far we have moved from pictograms to ideograms, then to sylla-baries, then to a kind of demotic or popular writing which used only consonants. The final stage came when speakers of Aryan tongues (more about what ' Aryan ' means in a later chapter) wrestled with a Semitic alphabet and found it wanting. It was the Greeks who introduced vowel-symbols and thus opened up the way to a very exact means of rendering spoken sounds. The vowel-symbols had their origin, like the rest of the alphabet, in old pictograms (see Fig. 8) ; Greek was content with seven :

$$\alpha \ \epsilon \ \eta \ \iota \ \upsilon \ \omega \ o$$

These letters are the so-called ' lower case ' forms. The peoples of Italy took the capital or ' upper case ' forms of five of these letters (they did not want η and ω) and thus equipped the Roman Empire that was to

L I O D   N N O K   R T H A R S

Read from right to left.

SR ATHR KONN DOIL = Sir Arthur Conan Doyle

M O H   K O L R SH

SHRLOK HOM

= Sherlock Holme(s)

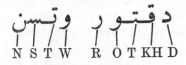

N S T W   R O T KH D

DKHTOR WTSN

= Doctor Watson

D R Y   D N L T O K S

SKOTLND YRD = Scotland Yard

لوور نوروود

Lower Norwood

Fig. 10.—English names taken from a translation of a Sherlock Holmes story into Malay. This is the Arabic alphabet in its *Jawi* (i.e. Eastern) form. Note that there are no capital letters, that fewer vowel signs are used than in the Roman alphabet (they are especially avoided before two consonants), and that what vowel letters there are perform two functions. و is /o/ or /u/ inside a word but /w/ at the beginning of a word ; /i/ and /e/ are shown by two inferior dots which also serve initially for /j/. The three vowel letters and ر are joined to a preceding letter but never to a following one. Most letters are given a calligraphic flourish at the end of a word.

come, along with its tributaries, with the tradition of the five vowels A, E, I, O, and V.

This question of upper and lower case letters (printers call them by these names because of the positions of the type-boxes that hold them) is too big to go into here. Arabic, we may note, has never had the tradition of small letters and capitals; the International Phonetic Alphabet gets on well enough with just lower case symbols. The original Roman alphabet was all capitals; small letters are a later development associated with a running or 'current' script, for capitals cannot easily be joined to each other. We would probably save much time and money if we followed the Arabic tradition of using small, or lower case, letters only. German insists on a capital initial for every noun; we all insist on capital initials for proper names, the beginning of a sentence, and abbreviations like UNO, NATO, USSR, and the rest. Also, in English, we have the egomania of a capital for the first personal pronoun. Archy, the cockroach that wrote poems on Don Marquis's typewriter, could not use capitals and still became a best-seller; the American poet e. e. cummings, though able to use a shift-key, still preferred lower case letters all the time.

The Roman alphabet spread all over the West, undergoing only slight modifications in the various colonial territories where it was used to write down the local language; the Greek alphabet was introduced into the non-Greek territories of Eastern Europe by more peaceful means than conquest. The present-day Russian alphabet resembles the Greek alphabet very closely; indeed, some letters are identical. St Cyril, a missionary of the ninth century A.D., took the Greek alphabet with him to the Slav territories he wished to convert to Christianity. Inevitably, it underwent modifications owing to the particular needs of Slav, and it became virtually a new alphabet—called, to this day, after the saint: the Cyrillic (in Russian, *Kirillitsa*) alphabet.

The world has now three great alphabets—the Roman, the Cyrillic, and the Arabic. The Roman and Cyrillic, even to the least trained observer, must seem to possess a common origin, but the Arabic looks like neither, nor does it resemble the Hebrew alphabet or the alphabets of India. Nevertheless, we can assert that all alphabets derive from the original Phoenician invention: the lack of consistency in writing or drawing the symbols, the tendency of each nation to develop its own quirks and create special letters to render its own idiosyncratic sounds —

Коммунистическая партия Советского Союза

ПРАВДА

**Орган Центрального Комитета
Коммунистической партии Советского Союза**

Fig. 11.—The title-box of the Russian newspaper *PRAVDA* (' TRUTH '). Above the name we read *Kommunisticheskaya Partiya Sovyetskovo Soyuza*. Note the palatalised vowels я (ya); e (ye) and ю (yu). The г of the third word is normally pronounced like the ' g ' is ' gas ', but in adjectival forms like this it becomes /v/. The phrase means ' Communist Party of the Soviet Union '. Below the title we read *Organ Tsyentral'novo Komityeta Kommunisticheskoi Partii Sovyetskovo Soyuza*. This seems fairly clear : ' Organ of the Central Committee of the Communist Party of the Soviet Union.' I have used an apostrophe to represent the ь in the second word. This symbol is a softener or palataliser of the preceding vowel. The encircled hero is, of course, Lenin.

HEADLINES FROM PRAVDA :

Манчестер рукоплещет Ю. Гагарину

Manchester rukopleshchet Yu. Gagarinu :
' Manchester acclaims Yu(ri) Gagarin '

ГАНГСТЕРИЗМ В ПОЛИТИКЕ США

Gangsterizm v Politikye S.Sh.A.
' Gangsterism in the Politics of the USA '

these are possible reasons for the eventual divergence of forms. But if we look closely at, say, the ' L ' symbol of Arabic, Greek, Russian, Hebrew, and the Roman alphabet, we cannot doubt the possession of common elements—two lines at an angle. The Roman ' S ' is a sort of snake ; so is the corresponding Arabic sign. Even the Arabic ' T ' symbol bears a ghostly resemblance to our own. The feeling that all alphabets are fundamentally one should ease our task in learning how to use the two great foreign alphabets. Whether or not we wish to learn the languages that these alphabets enshrine, sheer human curiosity should drive us to find out at least what the letters stand for. And to handle the Arabic alphabet is to be led into a little world of exquisite sensation.

COCA-COLA	STRIPTEASE	FOOTBALL
Кока-кола	*στριπτηζ*	*φυτπμολ*
Кока-кола	стриптиз	футбол
كوكا كولا	ستريفتيذ	فوتبول

ASPIRIN	GUINNESS	JAZZ
αστπιριν	*Γινις*	*διεζ*
аспирин	Гиннисс	джэз
اسفيرين	كينيس	جيذ

'International' words in (*a*) Roman, (*b*) Greek, (*c*) Cyrillic (or Russian), (*d*) Arabic ('Jawi' form) script.

(Note : in Modern Greek $\beta = /\beta/$; $\pi\mu$ is used for /b/.)

Fɪɢ. 12.

SEVEN

ADVENTURES OF AN ALPHABET

THE languages that have been most satisfied with the Roman alphabet as a set of phonemic signals are, inevitably, those that are derived from the Roman language—Italian, Spanish, Portuguese, French, Rumanian. The Roman alphabet fitted Latin like a glove, and it has fitted the dark-eyed daughters nearly as well, though French—language of dissent—has tended to chafe a little, introducing the gussets of diacritical helpers (acute and grave and circumflex and cedilla). The modern Latin tongues are so clearly agreed as to what the letters of the Roman alphabet signify, that we are able to deduce by comparison what they stood for in Latin : we can almost reproduce the very phonemes that Vergil, Horace, and Catullus juggled with. Thus, the letter ' i ' means /i/ in Paris, Madrid, Rome, Lisbon, Bucharest ; ' e ' means a half-close or half-open front vowel (/e/ or /ɛ/) ; ' o ' means a half-close or half-open back vowel (/o/ or /ɔ/) ; ' a ' can confidently be taken to stand for /a/ and ' u '—except in French—for /u/. It seems unlikely that they could have any widely differing meaning in the parent language. This family sticking-together with the vowels, this loyalty to the imperial mother, is not exactly matched with the consonants. If ' c ' means /k/ before ' a ' or ' o ' or ' u ', it does not always mean /s/ before ' i ' or ' e '. French opts for the /s/, Italian for /tʃ/, Castilian Spanish (but not provincial or South American) for /θ/. Nor do the Latin daughters agree about rendering the palatal ' n ' (/ɲ/). Portuguese has ' nh ', Spanish has ' ñ ', French and Italian have ' gn '. But, within the particular language, there is usually absolute consistency, so that French and Italian ' gn ' *always* mean /ɲ/, Spanish ' g ' before ' e ' or ' i ' *always* means /x/, Spanish ' ll ' and Portuguese ' lh ' *always* stand for /λ/.

But how about the Roman alphabet in England ? What has gone wrong here ? Why is it that no foreigner can say with any confidence, seeing a new English word in print, what the pronunciation is likely to be ? Why is the story of the Frenchman who drowned himself after reading ' Agatha Christie's Mousetrap Pronounced Success ' not really funny ? How has it come about that we can spell ' fish ' quite logically as ' photi ' (the ' ph ' in ' photo ', the ' o ' on ' women ', the ' ti ' in ' ration ') ? Why have we diverged so from common Continental agreement about the significance of the Roman letters ? That in itself would be tolerable if English spelling were consistent ; but English not only fails to agree with French, Spanish, Italian, and the rest—it fails to agree with itself. The only problem of learning English is the problem of spelling. If only English would say that ' xgyjpth ' stands for /i/ and ' zfrkhtgg ' stands for /u/ and be absolutely consistent about it, then there would be no problem for anyone—native or foreigner. It is the total lack of logic that is infuriating. How did it come about ? What can we do about it ?

We may as well begin with a piece of Anglo-Saxon or Old English. This ancestor of our present language was, very roughly speaking, used until the Normans settled in England and fertilised it with their brand of French. The following will only be intelligible to the lay reader if he is told that it is a translation of the Lord's Prayer ; it is very much a foreign language to us now :

Fæder ūre,
þū þe eart on heofonum,
sī þīn nama gehālgod.
Tōbecume þīn rīce.
Gewurþe ðin willa on eorðan swā swā on heofonum . . .

This is recognisably written with the Roman alphabet, but with certain letters that the Romans never used : the Germanic phonemes /θ/ as in ' thin ' and /ð/ as in ' then ' required special letters (the second of them, you will note, is used with its original Germanic value in the International Phonetic Alphabet). The letter ' þ ' (the Anglo-Saxons called it ' thorn ') was eventually to disappear, to be replaced (as was ' ð ') by the Frenchified ' th ', but it still survives as the first letter of ' þe Olde Englisshe Tea Shoppe '. It has been mistaken for ' Y ', but it certainly is not pronounced /j/. Along with these two consonant-letters, the Roman digraph ' æ ' (pronounced /ai/ in Latin) is used, representing the compromise sound in the Southern pronunciation of ' man ' a sound that is not quite an ' e ' and not quite an ' a '. Above certain vowel-letters appears the diacritic ' ¯ ', a symbol of vowel-length, but also a phonemic differentiator. The two phonemes /i/ and /ɪ/ would both appear as forms of the one phoneme /i/ to the Roman ear ; consequently, the Roman alphabet has only left the one letter ' i ' to represent them both. Anglo-Saxon ' ī ' stands for ' ee ' in ' see ' (/iː/) ; ' i ' stands for /ɪ/ (' willa ' is the ancestor of our modern ' will '). Already the Roman alphabet is being strained to meet the requirements of a non-Latin language. Add the fact that some unvoiced consonants tend to be voiced in Anglo-Saxon between two vowels, and we find that the ' f ' of ' heofonum ' (ancestor of modern ' heaven ') represents /v/.

Still, in the earliest stage of English, ' a ', ' e ', ' i ', ' o ', and ' u ' meant roughly what they still mean in the International Phonetic Alphabet and what they always meant in the Latin language. When we read Chaucer, we assume that these five vowels have *French* meanings, because ' ou '—following the new French custom—stands for /u/, and ' u ' seems to stand for /y/ in French *lune*. Roughly speaking, in the fourteenth century the following words had something like a Continental pronunciation : ' lady ', ' made ', ' name ' (/a/) ; ' house ', ' flour ' (/u/). The spellings of ' see ' and ' sea ' crystallise a half-close long vowel and a half-open long vowel respectively. Thus, the old pronunciation of ' see ' would be /seː/ and that of ' sea ' /sɛː/. The doubling of a letter to show length seems reasonable enough ; the addition of an ' a ' to show that a vowel is open rather than close is more subtle, but still logical. The same thing happens with back vowels. ' Moon ' shows a long close o-sound ; the pronunciation would be /moːn/. ' Road ' has an ' a ' after the ' o ' to indicate that the ' o ' is half-open or /ɔː/ (think of ' a ' after a vowel-letter as a ' tongue-down-a-bit ' signaller.) The long ' i ' (/iː/) which the Anglo-Saxons represented as ' ī ' is increasingly shown through the formula ' i + consonant + e = /iː/ ', so that words like ' shine ', ' fine ', ' mine ', etc., had, up to the end of the fourteenth century or perhaps later (one cannot be absolutely sure), the sound /iː/ in the middle.

The pronunciation of certain common English words in the mediaeval period can, then, be shown in relation to the Cardinal Vowel Chart as in Fig. 13. These long vowels use a Continental method of representation, helped out by doubling (' oo ' or ' ee ') to show length or an added ' a ' to show both length and half-open tongue-position. The chart (Fig. 13) looks incomplete because there is no word corresponding to Cardinal Vowel No. 5 (/ɑ/). It must be said that, in the history of spoken

English, that particular area of the mouth has been less important to speakers than to doctors. There are grounds for supposing that the use of the so-called long ' a ' (aaaaah) has always been limited and often sporadic. It does not exist in American English and, in England itself, it seems to be limited to East Midland English. Neither Chaucer nor Shakespeare knew it ; in the eighteenth century, a French word like *vase* had to be pronounced /vɔːz/ because /ɑː/ was not available, and

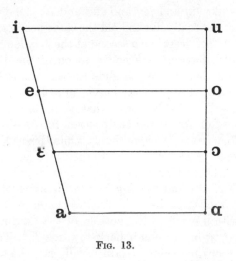

Fig. 13.

even the place-name ' Gibraltar ' came in as /dʒɪˈbrɔːltə/ because a Spanish ' a ' was too much like /ɑː/. It seems likely too that the corresponding rounded open back vowel—/ɒ/ as in ' hot '—has never really been pópular in England, and that something like /ɔ/ or even /ʌ/ has been preferred. Americans say ' hot ' as very nearly /hʌt/ ; Shakespeare's ' too, too solid flesh ' in *Hamlet* may have been more ' sullied ' than ' solid '. We can take it that, in most kinds of English up to, say, the end of the eighteenth century, the phoneme /aː/ was a pretty wide one, moving back to the borders of the territory of /ɑ/ and doing jobs that we now expect /ɑ/ to do.

So far we have established that the letters ' i ', ' e ', ' a ', ' ou ', ' oo ', ' oa ' for a long time represented ' Continental ' vowels in English, that an Italian or Spaniard coming to words like ' see ' or ' lady ' or ' moon ' in Chaucer's time would, giving the vowel letters the same value as in his own language, contrive—with a bit of extra vowel length—an exact English pronunciation. In other words, the Roman alphabet in England was still meaning pretty much what it meant to the rest of Europe. But, and we now remove our hats in the presence of a great mystery, a strange process began to operate in the English long vowels towards the end of the Middle Ages—a process known as a vowel shift.

Long vowels like /iː/ and /eː/ and /uː/ and /oː/ tend to be unstable. The tongue does not really like to hold the same position for a long time (which means, in fact, less than a second at the very longest) and so long vowels in English have always had a touch of the diphthong about them—the tongue has wanted to glide rather than stay still, holding the one long sound. Try pronouncing /iː/ in isolation, making it really long, and you will probably notice that your tongue wavers a little between the position for /i/ and the position for /ɪ/—in other words, it glides or diphthonguises. Now, probably while Henry V was fighting in France, the long /i/ of ' shine ' was ceasing to be long /i/ ; it was becoming unstable, turning into a diphthong, toppling from its high position (see Fig. 13) and moving in the direction of changing to a diphthong like /ai/. What has happened to the /iː/ in ' shine ' is that it has dropped with a crash to the bottom of the Cardinal Vowel Chart and become /a/ trying to climb back towards /i/. This is what the diphthong we know in ' shine ' (/ʃaɪn/) really is : the tongue trying to recover from its fall from /i/ to /a/ but never succeeding. Here, then, is the reason why ' shine ', ' fine ', ' tide ', ' my ' (which is really ' mij '— another way of writing /iː/) have the diphthong /aɪ/. There has been a change of sound, but the actual spelling still commemorates the pronunciation of the Middle Ages.

Now take another look at Fig. 13. With this vowel shift, ' shine ' no longer occupies the /i/ area of the mouth : there is a vacancy. ' See ' rises to fill the vacancy. What was /eː/ now becomes /iː/, and words like ' see ', ' fee ', ' keen ', ' reed ', ' weed ' have the /iː/ pronunciation we use to-day. But this movement upwards of ' ee ' leaves a vacancy. ' Sea ' rises to fill the vacancy, and the pronunciation is no longer /sɛː/ but /seː/.

Right up to the time of the French Revolution a distinction was made in the pronunciation of ' ee ' words and ' ea ' words. ' See ' was

/siː/ but ' sea ' was /seː/ ; ' feet ' was /fiˑt/ but ' feat ' was /feˑt/. ' Tea '
was always /teː/. The distinction is still made in Ireland ; indeed, the
Irish version of English is a sort of fossilisation of eighteenth-century
London speech. (Note again : the vowel shift gave ' speech ' as
/spiˑtʃ/ but ' speak ' as /speˑk/.)

With the rising of ' sea ' to the /e/ position, there is again a vacancy.
The /aː/ of ' lady ' rises to fill the vacancy, so that the Tudor pronunciation of ' lady ' was something like /lɛːdɪ/. Since the time of this great
vowel shift there has been another, so that, while words like ' see ' and
' feed ' have kept their /iː/, words like ' sea ' and ' read ' have risen to
join them, and ' see '/' sea ' ; ' tee '/' tea ' and the rest have become
homophones. The vacancy left by the rising of /seː/ to /siː/ has been
filled by words like ' lady ' and ' make ', whose /ɛː/ became /eː/. Eventually, /leːdɪ/ and /meˑk/ were diphthongised to /leɪdɪ/ and /meɪk/,
and this diphthong is there in most words with ' a + consonant + e '
at the present time—' fade ', ' trade ', ' cake ', ' fate ', and so on. Note
that some words with ' ea ' have lagged behind the others in the up-
ward shift, and so we have ' steak ' and ' break ' with /eɪ/ in them
(/eː/ in Ireland) instead of the expected /iː/ (though some Welshmen
pronounce ' steak ' as /stiˑk/). This explains the fact that ' break '
rhymes with ' make ' to-day, but in Shakespeare's time rhymed with
' speak '. It also explains some of the foreigner's difficulties in learning
English from a book.

The vowel shift that took place with the long front vowels also took
place with the long back vowels. The Anglo-Saxon ' hūs ' and ' mūs '
were shown in the Middle Ages as ' house ' and ' mouse ' because, as
in French, the letter ' u ' was required to represent the front rounded
vowel /y/. With the general shift, ' house ' ceased to be /huːs/ and
dropped to a diphthongal state like ' shine '—/a/ trying to climb back
towards the high vowel but not succeeding. And so ' house ' was
pronounced, and still is, as /haʊs/, though some Scots still prefer
/huˑs/. The vacancy left by the shift of ' house ' to diphthongal status
was speedily filled by ' moon ' ; this ceased to be /moːn/ and became
/muːn/—the pronunciation it has to-day. ' Road ' rose to fill the gap
left by the rising of the ' moon ', and so the old pronunciation /roːd/
was changed to /roːd/. Diphthonguisation gives us our present pronunciation /roʊd/.

This strange behaviour of the long English vowels at the close of the

mediaeval period has resulted in the ' un-Continental ' spelling system
we have, or part of it. The instability of vowels is, as we have seen,
partly a consequence of their length, and with languages like Spanish
and Italian, which tend to specialise in short vowels, we may expect a
vowel-letter to mean what it meant to a Roman. With the short vowels
of English—such as /ɪ/ in ' bit ', /ɛ/ in ' men ', /ʊ/ in ' full '—there has
been less tendency to change, and so the letter values have been more
or less maintained over the centuries. Still, there remains the puzzle of
the vowel /ʌ/ in ' mother ', ' son ', ' sun ', the lack of a consistent
symbol for it. It has never had a letter of its own, any more than
/ə/ has,' precisely because it is a comparatively new sound (some
dialects of English, such as Lancashire, still do not accept it), sprung
into being long after the period of adapting the Roman alphabet to the
needs of English. The phoneme /ʊ/ represents the traditional short
u-sound, still flourishing in words like ' put ', ' pull ', ' push ', ' full '.
It also appears in words like ' foot ', ' wool ', ' should ', where the
shortening of a long /u/ also brought a slight lowering and advancing
of the tongue (/ʊ/, we remember, is a little lower and a little further
forward than /u/). Our modern /ʌ/ is a sound made with spread lips,
representing an unrounding of a back vowel like /o/ or /ʊ/. If we think
of it as the phoneme that results from pronouncing a short back vowel
with lips spread instead of pursed or rounded, then we have a good
rough general picture of it.

If the letter ' u ' can stand for /ʊ/ as in ' pull ', /ʌ/ as in ' cut ', and
keep its traditional Roman vowel in ' blue ', it can also seem to do
fantastic things in words like ' bury ' and ' busy '. We are reminded
here that, like French, English had a rounded high front vowel (as in
lune or Chaucer's ' vertu ') which the Anglo-Saxons, like users of the
IPA, represented as ' y '. The unrounding and lowering of this /y/ will
easily explain ' busy ' as /bɪzɪ/ and ' bury ' as /bɛrɪ/. The reader can play
the game of deciding why ' what ', ' war ', ' swan ' and similar words
have ' a ' representing /ɔ/ or /ɒ/. He will find the answer in the semi-
vowel /w/ or /ʍ/ preceding the vowel : the lip-rounding associated with
these two sounds is transferred to the following vowel. This business
of one sound's influence on another, the tendency to assimilate, has
much to do with the disparity between the way we pronounce and the
way we spell. The normal plural ending '-s' stands for either /s/ or /z/,
according to whether the preceding sound is unvoiced or voiced (e.g.

' cats ', ' ducks ', ' snakes ' have /s/, but ' dogs ', ' pigs ', ' birds ' have /z/). This is a trick the foreign student of English has to learn with no real assistance from the *look* of the word.

Consonants have not undergone such violent changes as vowels (especially long vowels), and a consonant letter in English can often be expected to give approximate guidance (in terms of the mother alphabet) to the sound it stands for. Digraphs like ' th ' and ' sh ' and ' ch ' have had to be specially made for English ; the last two are consistent, but ' th ' gives no indication as to whether a voiced sound or unvoiced sound is meant. Still, a consonant letter normally signals the presence of a consonantal sound, with certain exceptions. The digraph ' gh ' is a memorial to a departed /x/ (an unvoiced velar fricative as in ' loch ' or ' Bach '). ' Light ', ' bright ', ' right ', and the rest retain an unvoiced semi-vowel (/ç/) in their Scots pronunciation (' It's a braw bricht moonlicht nicht '), but the ' gh ' is merely an indicator of diphthonguisation (igh = /aɪ/) in Queen's English. In words like ' taught ', ' caught ', ' bought ', it is an indicator of length (/ɔː/), though an unnecessary one, for ' taut ' and ' taught ' are both pronounced /tɔ·t/. In ' laugh ' and ' cough ' it means /f/, and in ' hiccough ', by a mistaken analogy with ' cough ', it disguises a /p/.

The English ' r ' was once the signaller of a good strong trill, but it now (in Queen's English) stands for a weak fricative before or between vowels. In words like ' fire ', ' more ', ' there ', ' moor ', ' beer ' it merely stands for the central vowel /ə/. In words like ' girl ', ' word ', ' hurl ' it means that the preceding vowel is /ɜː/. In ' far ', ' card ', ' cord ' it acts as a mere signaller of length (/fɑː/ ; /kɑːd/ ; /kɔːd/).

Certain consonants are silent because they only act as visual pointers to the foreign derivation of the word which contains them, as with ' psychology ', ' yacht ', ' debt ' (Latin *debitum*). ' Ch ' ceases to mean /tʃ/ when it appears in a word that comes from Greek, like ' chaos ' or ' chorus '. But, on the whole, the tricks of English consonantal representation are easily learned.

The reader will now have seen enough of vowel change in English (there is, of course, far, far more) to know that English has been a highly changeable language and that the alphabet has been very slow to accommodate itself to change. Our vowel symbols (and some of our consonantal ones) give a picture of how the language used to be pronounced—as much as six or seven hundred years ago. The development of new sounds with no corresponding invention of new symbols also helps to explain our spelling chaos. But there are other factors, too. Seventeenth-century pedants stuck unnecessary letters into words merely to show the origin in Greek or Latin : 'debt' and 'doubt' are fine examples. In Shakespeare's time, and after, there was no agreed system of spelling : you could spell as you pronounced, or as you thought you pronounced. Before the invention of movable type, this was a godsend to printers. To ' justify ' a line (i.e., to fill it out to the right-hand margin) they would add odd unnecessary letters, turning ' dog ' to ' dogg ' or even ' dogge '. This practice ended before movable type came in, partly as a result of the development of the news-sheet during the Civil War, when compositors had no time to make their pages look pretty, with neat margins, and tended to use the same spelling for any given word each time that word appeared. Standardisation of spelling was partly Dr Johnson's achievement (one of so many), hammered home with the bulk of his incredible Dictionary.

We all tend now to spell in the same way ; we admit there are such things as ' spelling mistakes ' and we are prepared to be penalised for making them. Private letters, however, will often break the rules and breathe that old freedom of the Elizabethan days. I have an educated correspondent who recently spelt ' Sealyham ' as ' Celium ' and ' coat of arms ' as ' court of arms ' (the latter shows that she pronounces ' coat ' as /kɔ·t/ ; it is a pointer to the fact that she is Welsh). Such ' phonetic ' spelling would, if recorded sound did not exist, be a valuable guide to a posterity looking for the facts of twentieth-century pronunciation : we ourselves owe a vast amount of our knowledge of English sound-changes to the letters of the past. Despite the existence of ' public ' spelling rules, however, and our general acceptance of standards, we are not happy about English spelling and are always talking of doing something to change it.

Innumerable suggestions have been made, often by people untrained in linguistics, and George Bernard Shaw is but one of many who have sponsored—in life or from the grave—a ' rational ' spelling scheme for English. Shaw's *Androcles and the Lion* has just, at this moment of writing, appeared in improved spelling ; a modified phonetic alphabet is already in use in some schools. British units of money and mensuration may soon, we are promised or threatened, be brought into line with Continental practice ; would it be wise to take the plunge and give to the English alphabet something of the consistency possessed by the alphabets of Europe ? There are many reasons for being cautious about the taking of such a radical step.

The rationalisation of English spelling means to many people only one thing—spelling English ' phonetically ', making each symbol used stand for one sound and one sound only, achieving absolute consistency in our written or printed symbols. Is such consistency possible without losing the semantic identity of the word itself ? For, to take a simple example, ' the ' is /ðə/ before a consonant and /ði/ before a vowel ; sometimes the indefinite article is, in very deliberate American speech, pronounced /eɪ/ ; most often, though, it is /ə/. The pronunciation of any word will vary according to the emphasis it is given within a certain context. If the word is, to the eye, always to be the same word, an exact phonetic rendering is not really desirable.

Attempts to bring spelling of English words in line with the values of the mother alphabet depend on which pronunciation is to be considered ' correct ' or standard. The Queen's English rendering of the diphthong in ' rain ' is /eɪ/, and to spell it as ' ei ' seems reasonable : Eliza Doolittle's test-piece would then be ' The rein in Spein steiz meinly in the pleinz '. But is it fair to impose this rendering on those elements of the reading population who do not use this diphthong ? ' Rain ' is a more rational spelling than ' rein ' to the Cockney, whose diphthong approaches /aɪ/ or /æɪ/. Northerners say /reːn/ or /rɛːn/. What can be done about eliminating the letter ' r ' in words like ' park ', ' dark ', and so on ? There is no corresponding sound in Queen's English, which uses /pɑ·k/ and /dɑ·k/, but a host of other English dialects—including the various forms of American English—use some allophone or other of the /r/-phoneme. Like Chinese, the written form of English has to serve for a great number of spoken forms, so that ' father ' means /fɑːðə/ or /faːðə/ or /fæːðr/ or /fɛːðər/ or /faːvə/, according to class or region. There is a lot to be said for regarding our existing English spelling as part phonetic and part ideographic : we get some idea of the sound of the word, but we chiefly regard the word as a visual shape suggesting a bundle of phonemes which carries an accepted meaning.

Any changes we wish to make in English spelling ought, perhaps, to be limited to the consonants ; to legislate for the vowels of the entire

English-speaking world is presumptuous, for no standard spoken form of the language can ever be universally imposed. But even if we eliminate ' gh ' from ' light ' and ' night ' we are depriving the Scots of a consonantal pointer ; moreover, we shall have to create a new convention to show that ' i ' is pronounced /aɪ/ and not /ɪ/. The allegedly vulgar American ' nite ' is sensible enough ; but is it worth while taking all this trouble for a mere handful of words containing ' gh ' ? I would, as I have previously indicated, be glad to see a more consistent use of ' z ', creating unambiguous forms like ' boyz ', ' birdz ', ' scizzorz ' (or ' sizzorz '). I should like ' dh ' to be used for the voiced form of ' th ', so that ' thin ' could be set against ' dhen ' and ' thought ' against ' dhough '. (Incidentally, one would not object to the spelling ' dho ' for this latter ; unfortunately, nearly all one's proposals for spelling reform are of this small and niggardly order—too insignificant to mean very much in the great disorderly jungle of English orthography.)

There is a very strong argument against a ' phonetic ' spelling for those words that derive from Greek and Latin—an argument which consults the foreign learner rather than the native schoolchild. ' Education ', ' situation ', ' edifice ', and other Romance words are near-identical in spelling to their forms in the modern Romance languages. The learner of English whose native word is *éducation* or *educacion* or *educazione* will hardly see something like ' edyukeishun ' as familiar ; the existing English spelling, though it may give no clue to pronunciation, is at least intelligible as a written symbol. And even when one considers the proposal to drop the ' k ' in ' knife ' as altogether reasonable, one is brought up short with the realisation of how much this spelling helps the Frenchman with a *canif* in his pocket.

Should we leave well alone ? On the whole, yes. Sort out a few minor irrationalities but leave the great horrible bulk of our spelling untouched : much of it is a link with Europe, all of it is a link with our past. To understand how our spelling comes about is to forgive it. Let us make the fullest possible use of the International Phonetic Alphabet as an auxiliary, both in our English schools and in our classes for foreigners ; if we want to show what the phonemes of our language are, here at least is a scientific way of doing it. But let us not exaggerate the difficulties of English spelling ; let us merely be more tolerant of innocent transgressions, not always ready to bang a gong like a spelling-bee master. Nobody wants a 'silent' correction of Jane Austen's *Love and Freindship*. A guage works as well as a gauge, and parralell lines still meet at infinity. GCE examiners should have more important things to look for than offences against orthographical rectitude.

It remains to say that some people—including some teachers—have seriously proposed that we solve all our problems of spelling by letting the pronunciation follow the orthography rather than vice versa. I have heard a teacher try to teach the pronunciation of 'cabbage' as 'cab age' because of this mystical belief in the primacy of the visual form. On such people may the gods of language have a cruel revenge. Such a sin is the ultimate one of exalting the shadow above the substance, the appearance over the reality.

D

EIGHT

WORDS

1

For the moment—but only for the moment—it will be safe to assume that we all know what is meant by the word ' word '. I may even consider that my typing fingers know it, defining a word (in a whimsical conceit) as what comes between two spaces. The Greeks saw the word as the minimal unit of speech ; to them, too, the atom was the minimal unit of matter. Our own age has learnt to split the atom and also the word. If atoms are divisible into protons, electrons, and neutrons, what are words divisible into ?

Words as things uttered split up, as we have already seen, into phonemes, but phonemes do not take *meaning* into account. We do not play on the phonemes of a word as we play on the keys of a piano, content with mere sound ; when we utter a word we are concerned with the transmission of meaning. We need an appropriate kind of fission, then—one that is *semantic*, not *phonemic*. Will division into syllables do ? Obviously not, for syllables are mechanical and metrical, mere equal ticks of a clock or beats in a bar. If I divide (as for a children's reading primer) the word ' metrical ' into ' met-ri-cal ', I have learned nothing new about the word : these three syllables are not functional as neutrons, protons, electrons are functional. But if I divide the word as ' metr- ; -ic ; -al ' I have done something rather different. I have indicated that it is made of the root ' metr- ', which refers to measurement and is found in ' metronome ' and, in a different phonemic disguise, in ' metre ', ' kilometre ', and the rest ; ' -ic ', which is an adjectival ending found also in ' toxic ', ' psychic ', etc., but can some-times indicate a noun, so that ' metric ' itself can be used in· a phrase like ' Milton's metric ' with full noun status ; ' -al,' which is an un-ambiguous adjectival ending, as in ' festal ', ' vernal ', ' partial '. I have split ' metrical ' into three contributory forms which (remem-bering that Greek *morph-* means ' form ') I can call *morphemes*.

Let us now take a collocation of words—a phrase or sentence—and attempt a more extended analysis. This will do : ' Jack's father was eating his dinner very quickly.' Here I would suggest the following fission : (1) ' Jack ' ; (2) ' -'s ' ; (3) ' father ' ; (4) ' was ' ; (5) ' eat ' ; (6) ' -ing ' ; (7) ' hi- ' ; (8) ' -s ' ; (9) ' dinner ' ; (10) ' very ' ; (11) ' quick ' ; (12) ' -ly '—making a total of twelve morphemes. ' Jack ' can exist on its own, but the addition of ' -'s ' (a morpheme denoting possession) turns a proper noun into an adjective. ' Father ' cannot be reduced to smaller elements, for, though ' -er ' is an ending common to four nouns of family relationship, ' fath- ' on its own has no more meaning than ' moth- ' or ' broth-' or ' sist- '. ' Eat' can be an infinitive or imperative, but the suffix ' -ing ' makes it into a present participle. ' Hi- ' signals an aspect of the singular masculine personal pronoun, but it can have no real meaning until it is completed by the objective ending ' -m ' or, as here, the ' -s ' denoting possession. ' Dinner ' is indivisible, for ' din ' on its own belongs to a very different semantic area, and to use ' din ' for ' dinner ' (as some facetious people do) or to make a duplicated child's form ' din din ' is merely to use a truncated form of a whole word, implying the prior existence of that word. Finally, ' quick ' is an adjective ; the morpheme ' -ly ' turns it into an adverb.

It will be seen from the above that morphemes fall into two classes. There are those which cannot stand on their own but require to be combined with another morpheme before they can mean anything— like ' -'s ', ' -ing ', ' hi- ', ' -ly '. We can call these *bound forms*, or *helper morphemes*. The other morphemes are those which can stand on their own, conveying a meaning, and these can be called *free forms* or *semantemes* (' meaning-forms '). ' Jack ', ' father ', ' was ', ' eat ', ' dinner ', ' quick ' are of this order : these are simple free forms, because they cannot be subdivided into smaller elements. But words like ' Jack's ', ' his ', ' quickly ' *can* be subdivided, each into either (*a*) a free form + a bound form or (*b*) two bound forms (like ' hi- ' and ' -s ').

I have used the term ' word ' so far without attempting a definition, yet the fact that we have been able to analyse words into morphemes shows that we are finding no difficulty in recognising a word. But the time has come for definition, and the great Bloomfield, who may be regarded as the father of modern linguistic theory, suggested that a word was a ' minimum free form ', meaning a form unlimited as to the number of bound forms or ' helper morphemes ' but strictly limited to one free form only. This would make words of ' John ' (one free form), ' John's ' (one free form and one bound form), ' its ' (the same), ' his ' (two bound forms adding up to one free form). It would not, however, make words of compounds like ' penknife ', ' manhole-cover ' or German *Geheimestaatspolízei* (' Secret-state-police ' or ' Gestapo '). There would have to be a new term, such as ' word-compound ', to cover these and the following fantastic verb coined by Robert Browning :

' While treading down rose and ranunculus,
You Tommy-make-room-for-your-uncle us.'

But these compounds frequently set into what are, at least phonemically, simple entitities—' breakfast ' (/brɛkfst/, not ' break fast ') ; ' cupboard ' (/kʌbəd/, not ' cup board ') ; ' bo's'n ', not ' boatswain '. It is difficult to draw the line, and the need for Bloomfield's limited definition is not at all clear : a compound word is still a word, doing a word's job.

Bloomfield also said that a free form could be recognised by its ability to stand as a complete utterance—granted, of course, a context of other words or of pure situation which would make the meaning of the isolated free form quite clear. Thus, we can take words from our sentence ' Jack's father was eating his dinner very quickly ' and demonstrate this thesis without too much strain :

' Whose is that cap ? ' ' *Jack's*.'
' *Father !* ' (The speaker is calling.)
' She *is* pretty, isn't she ? ' ' *Was*.'
' What's he doing now ? ' ' *Eating*.'
' Whose book will you borrow ? ' ' *His*.'
' Why have you come ? What do you want ? ' ' *Dinner*.'
' Ugly, isn't he ? ' ' *Very*.'
' *Quickly !* ' (The speaker gives an errand-goer a shove.)

The trouble with this is that a breakdown occurs with the indefinite articles ' a ' and ' an ' and the definite article ' the '. These can only make complete statements in a context of language, not of life : it is the words themselves that are referred to, not—as with the above examples—what the words stand for. Thus, ' What word did you use then ? ' ' " The ".'—' Do you say " a " or " an " before " hotel " ? ' ' " An ".'

It seems that, if Bloomfield's thesis is to hold so far, we must regard the articles as bound forms, forms incapable of acting on their own— that is to say, not as words at all. Not all languages possess a definite article, but some that do seem unable to regard it is a separate word. Rumanian has a newspaper called *Timpul* (' The Times ') ; the original Latin was *Tempus illud,* but now the remains of the *illud* act as an article glued to the end of the noun. The same glueing of an article to the end of a word is found in Aztec—*tomatl* ; *chocolatl ; Quetzlcoatl ; Popacatapetl.* Arabic glues its article to the front, as in our own Arabic loan-words ' alchemy ', ' algebra ', ' alcohol ', ' apricot ' (*al-praecoq*), in *Al-Sultan,* even in the holy name *Allah.* (Note that the great Alexander appears in Arabic as Al-Iskander ; the ' Al ' is assumed to be an article and removed to leave ' Iskander '—a common Muslim name.) English itself has timidly played with the glue-pot: ' an adder ' should be ' a nadder ', ' an apron ' was once ' a napron ', and ' an orange ' ought to be, as in Spanish, ' a norange ' (*una naranja*).

So, if the articles—' the ', ' a ', ' an '—are bound forms, they cannot be words ; yet we say they *are* words : they have space before and behind ; they are defined in dictionaries. Evidently something is wrong somewhere. For that matter, something seems to be wrong with the limitation of ' single-word sentences ' to bound forms. If a pupil says, ' I came quick,' and the teacher utters the chiding correction ' " -Ly " ', then an error of usage is being corrected : the referent of ' -ly ' is itself. But if a man says, ' It's been ages since I saw you. I'll just run up to the nursery and take a look at your son,' the proud parents can answer : ' -s ! ' (/zzzzz/), meaning ' We've more than one son now ! ' In other words, that bound form the plural suffix can refer, not to mere accidence (the correct inflection of a word), but to something in the real, external world—' more than one son '.

I suggest that we allow the morpheme in its two forms—the morpheme expressing meaning ; the morpheme which merely helps to modify meaning or create larger structures—to rest as our scientific unit. The term ' word ' cannot have any *significant* denotation : a word is what my typing fingers think it is—a cluster of symbols or even a single symbol separated by space from other clusters or single symbols. The symbols represent phonemes. The words of connected speech do not even have the frame of silence around them : they are all glued together in a single act of communication. But it is convenient to assume that words have real existence and even to create a science of word-study called *lexicology* (not to be confused with *lexicography*, which is the harmless drudgery of dictionary-making). Not delving too deeply into what a word is, we are able to embrace the single phoneme /ə/ (the indefinite article ' a ') or /o/ (French for ' water '— *eau*) as easily as the word-monsters of the so-called agglutinative languages : *nakomajn'ytamjun'n'ybolamyk*, for instance, which, according to W. J. Entwistle (*Aspects of Language*, 1953), is the Koryat for ' They're always telling lies to us ' (Koryat is spoken in Siberia). It appears to be a good language for telegrams.

2

GET ready for two new fearsome technical terms. Looking at words, we soon become aware that they fall into two rough categories—words that mean something when in isolation, like ' apple ', ' gramophone ', ' tulip ' ; words that only possess meaning when combined with other words in phrases or sentences—such as ' it ', ' and ', ' if ', ' or '. These are, of course, analogous to the two types of morpheme that can exist within the word itself, like the free form ' eat ' and the bound form ' -ing ' in ' eating '. So in the statement ' The orange is yellow ', we can pick out ' orange ' and ' yellow ' as words which carry meaning if chalked up singly or written in the sky by sky-writing aircraft. These free forms, because they possess independent meaning, are called *auto-semantic* words. ' The ' and ' is ', on the other hand, mean nothing outside the context of a sentence ; they only develop meaning when we make a synthesis of them with words like ' orange ' and ' yellow '. We can say that they are *synsemantic*.

But can a word really possess meaning outside a context ? Are not perhaps all words really synsemantic ? Having read the sentence ' The orange is yellow', you will have a clear enough image of a fruit which is juicy within and yellow without. But if the word ' orange ' were suddenly to be written on the sky by an aircraft, would we—without the assistance of other words—really be sure of its meaning ? Certain contexts or associations might fix ' orange ' as a fruit (oranges are regularly advertised through various media), but the word might merely mean a colour. In Liverpool, ' ORANGE ' painted on a wall might have completely different associations—William of Orange, the

Orange Lodges, the Battle of the Boyne—and the citrous element would be expunged by the political. Similarly, ' yellow ' without a context hovers between the colour and the adjective meaning ' cowardly '. Indeed, one can think of few words that are genuinely autosemantic, and these are not necessarily autosemantic in every language. ' Milk ' in English is unambiguous enough, but *leche* in Spanish can be an insult, and *susu* in Malay can mean as much the source of the milk as the milk itself. This is as much as to say that no single thing in the non-linguistic world is capable of preserving the word attached to it from vagueness, imprecision, ambiguity.

Though one may except proper names—words or word-groups signifying some unique natural or human referent : ' the Taj Mahal ' ; ' William Ewart Gladstone ' ; ' *La Bohème* ' ; ' the English Channel ' ; ' Ben Nevis ' ; ' Brigitte Bardot ' ; ' Lolita.' Yet these names only strictly come within the field of the lexicologist (and the lexicographer, for that matter) when they start to shed their particular denotation. If a girl is called a ' proper little Lolita ', then ' Lolita ' is turning into a common noun—a word expressive of a whole class instead of a single fictitious character. Indeed, proper names do not really possess a meaning at all : they are arbitrary signs, mere laundry marks. What does the name ' Theodore ' mean ? Its *etymology* (etymology deals with word-origin) is Greek, and the Greek words which make up the name mean ' God's gift ', but this tells us nothing about the person or persons to whom the name is attached. (Etymology, one may say now, has nothing to do with the meaning of any word. ' Silly ' is derived from Anglo-Saxon ' saelig '—' happy, blessed, holy '—but this etymology does not help us to fix the present-day meaning of the word.) ' Theodore,' then, means all people called Theodore, taking the widest context ; taking the narrowest, it means all the people called Theodore whom we happen to know or know about.

The science of meaning is called *Semantics*, and it deals with language at those points where it is closest to the ' real world '. The phonetician and grammarian tend to lock themselves in their laboratories, but the semantic specialist is close to the very roots of thought and action. George Orwell, in his novel *Nineteen Eighty-four*, saw how it might be possible for semantic control of language to change the whole pattern of a society. ' Newspeak ' is the official language of Ingsoc (' English Socialism '), and its limitation of the field of possible linguistic expression aims at making heterodox opinion impossible : political rebellion cannot be conceived in the mind, for the semantic elements of dissidence do not exist. If ' bad ' means ' opposed to the principles of Ingsoc ', and Big Brother is the eternal personification of these principles, then a statement like ' Big Brother is bad ' is absurd ; it is like saying ' x = not-x '. In the totalitarian societies of our day we have seen how meaning can be delimited to serve the ends of the Party ; but even in free societies we are perpetually bombarded by semantic perversions—mainly from politicians and advertisers, whose interests are furthered by the distortion or delimiting of meaning. ' The pacific uses of the H-Bomb ' is as absurd as the Orwellian ' War is Peace ' ; ' peace offensive ' is a phrase I have heard on the radio ; ' X is a man's smoke ' is a deliberate exploitation of a limited area of connotation ; ' It's the ice-cream treat of the TV age ' does not really admit of analysis.

Semantics is so big and important a subject that, in the few decades of its acknowledged existence as a science, it has already built up its own vast polyglot library. The book by Ogden and Richards—*The Meaning of Meaning*—states in its title what the basic inquiry of Semantics is ; it is an inquiry which may well go on for ever. We all use words ; do we know how tentative, complex, and fundamentally dangerous it is to commit even the simplest statement to the air ? A friend says to me, ' I like cats ' ; I say that I understand his meaning. But once I start to analyse I find myself plunging into a world where things seem neither intelligible nor necessary : what is ' I ', what is ' like ', what is ' cats ' ? I am drawn into ontology, psychology, physiology, zoology, and I end doubting the existence of everything, including the possibility of language's possessing any sense-potentialities at all.

One thing we can be fairly sure about is that a word—a ' phonemic event '—only exists at all because of some entity that has prior existence in the non-linguistic world. This non-linguistic world may be seen as having two aspects : first, there are the things to which language ultimately refers—' real ' events or objects, which we assume have a life of their own ; second, there is an area of mind where the speaker and hearer (or writer and reader) meet to agree on some interpretation of the real event or object. Thus, at one end we have the *word*, at the other we have the *referent*, in the middle we have the *sense*. The referent is perhaps a matter for the philosopher ; the word is certainly the linguist's concern ; the sense interests everybody, from the logician to the literary critic.

Whether the referent of a word really (in the sense of ' demonstrably ') exists is no concern of ours. We may talk about the attributes of God even though some would say that God's existence has not been satisfactorily proved. We may talk about the characters of a novel, knowing that these exist only in a very special sense—certainly not as the Albert Memorial or Red Square exists. A hypothesis may have a mental existence and the ginger-and-white cat that sits by me at this moment of writing may have a physical one : to the user of words they inhabit the same area of reference. Ultimately, of course, even the most abstract idea must go back to something in the world of sense, so that the notion of God may derive from tree-spirits, which themselves are an attempt to explain the outward manifestations of a tree's life. I repeat : this is no concern of our present study, though we cannot help being curious about referents. After all, Dr Johnson said in the preface to his Dictionary : ' I am not yet so lost in lexicography, as to forget that words are the daughters of earth, and that things are the sons of heaven.'

A speaker speaks a word ; a hearer hears it. If he understands the word he has stepped into the same area of sense as the speaker. The meaning of a word, then, may be thought of as this common area of meeting. But the sense, it goes without saying, depends on the referent, and the nature of the referent has to be defined by the context. Thus, the ' cat ' of ' The cat sat on the mat ' is different from the ' cat ' of ' Bring back the cat for thugs and rapists '. We cannot say that ' cat ' is a single word possessing two distinct meanings ; there are two words phonemically identical but semantically different : we call these *homonyms*. The ' cat ' of the second sentence refers back etymologically—by the grim fancy of ' cat o' nine tails '—to the cat of the hearthrug, but word-origin can never be invoked, as we have already pointed out, in the examination of meanings.

But what makes words less precise than mathematical symbols is their tendency to suggest meanings other than the ones intended in particular limited contexts. The definition of context is often not enough ; many words tremble at various frontiers of sense ; ambiguity is a vice of words. Ambiguity comes about not merely through homonymity, but through metaphorical extension (which may or may not lie behind homonymity, as with ' cat '), and through the fact that words attempt two opposing jobs—particularisation and generalisation. ' Cat ' will describe a new-born kitten and a fully-grown tiger, so that opposite notions (weakness, strength ; tame, wild ; tiny, huge) are contained in the same word. ' I love fish ' can have opposed meanings ; Shakespeare makes Henry V say that he loves France so well that he will not part with a single province of it. It is, indeed, only with the poet or imaginative prose-writer that language functions smoothly. Ambiguity ceases to be a vice ; its deliberate exploitation is revelled in. There are layers of meaning, all relevant to the context. Homonyms become deliberate puns—not necessarily comic. Lady Macbeth will *gild* the faces of the grooms with blood, ' for it must seem their *guilt*.' ' Die ' in *Romeo and Juliet* means what it says, but also means to experience the sexual orgasm. ' Reasons,' to Falstaff, can be plentiful as blackberries (' reasons ' = /reːznz/ = ' raisins '). A scientific age like our own tends to worry about this aspect of language. Some readers of a novel of mine were unhappy about the title, *The Worm and the Ring* : they wanted to know what it really meant. It meant, I told them, sexual incapacity, the failure of a marriage because of the moral weakness of the husband, the lowliness of crawling things, and the golden round of heaven, the Wagnerian myth (*Wurm* = dragon). They were dissatisfied : meaning should be mathematical, unambiguous. But this plurality of reference is in the very nature of language, and its management and exploitation is one of the joys of writing.

Words tend not merely to be ambiguous but to be emotional. ' Mother ' has a clear dictionary meaning (a *denotation*), but, because of the filial status shared by all men, it is drenched in associations of strong feeling, it has powerful emotional *connotations*. Thus, ' mother ' may be attached to a country or a college ('motherland'; *alma mater*) so that appropriate attitudes of loyalty may be induced in citizens or alumni. But the connotations can be wiped out completely in a term like ' mother-of-pearl ', which is as cold as ' matrix '. This has much to do with the distribution of emphasis : ' pearl ' is the stressed element and the rest of the compound is pronounced weakly : /mʌðərəv 'pɜːl/. The same process is at work in ' This is the BBC Home Service ', where the highly emotive ' home ' is given less stress than the following word. As ambiguity may be used by advertisers and demagogues to confuse or deceive, so that emotional connotations of words like

' England ', ' children ', ' duty ' can be exploited in wartime oratory or in bad poetry at any time. Words like these are assured of a ' stock response' in the unwary reader; the bad poet lets emotive associations do his work for him.

It follows from what I have said that the learning of foreign languages involves more than the amassing of denotations, the taking in of primary meanings only. *Fille* and *baiser*, which seem to mean ' girl ' and ' to kiss ' respectively in French, are notoriously dangerous words to use. *Buang ayer* in Malay means literally ' to throw water ' but has taken on a particular gross meaning ; *bulan* in the same language can mean primarily ' moon ' or ' month ' but also, by a natural extension, ' menstruation.' One has to watch context all the time. Meaning resides shadowily in the morpheme, less so in the word, less so again in the phrase or sentence or paragraph ; but meaning only comes to its fullest flower in the context of an entire way of life.

3

EVERYTHING flows, including language, and one of the difficulties we meet with in the study of meaning is the fact that meanings change. There are various reasons for this—some essentially linguistic, others psychological or historical. *Pas* means ' step ' in French, and *ne . . . pas* means ' not ' (literally : ' not a step '). Because *pas* is associated with the negative *ne*, it has taken on a negative meaning of its own, as in *Pas moi*—' not me '. This, the effect of association, is entirely a linguistic cause of semantic change.

But most changes take place because society changes—either in its attitude to life or in its formal institutions. ' Parliament ' does not mean for us what it meant in the Middle Ages, because the institution which is the referent of the word has changed radically. Hamlet, talking about actors, refers to the ' humorous man '—not the comedian, but the emotional actor : the old theory of humours (the primary fluids of the body which, according to the proportions of their mixture, determined a man's temperament) has long gone, but left this word behind to take on a different meaning. It is not long since ' atom ' meant what it meant to the Greeks—' what could not further be divided'. The word can no longer mean that, but we retain it. Inertia, conservatism will ensure that a word remains in the vocabulary, but change of meaning will be enforced by the non-conservative elements in man himself.

We cannot examine all types of semantic change here, but we can note the tendency of words to move from a wider to a narrower range of meaning. For instance, ' fowl ' once meant any kind of bird but now only means a chicken ; ' hound ' was once any kind of dog but its meaning is (except in a jocular sense) now strictly limited ; a deer was once ' beast in general '. All these words retain the older meaning in their modern German form : *Vogel ; Hund ; Tier*. ' Meat,' once any kind of food, is now restricted to what comes from the butcher, though the older sense is fossilised in ' sweetmeat '. The opposite process—expansion of meaning instead of restriction—is rarer ; perhaps the change in meaning of ' bird ' (which once meant merely a young bird) is due to the limiting of the meaning of ' fowl '.

Sometimes a limitation of meaning will be associated with a sort of value-judgement, so that ' smelly ' refers only to a bad smell. We can call this a pejorative change and note some very peculiar examples. Italian, for instance, derives its word for ' bad '—*cattivo*—from the Latin word for a prisoner, *captivus*. A cretin is, etymologically, a Christian. A knave was merely a boy (German *Knabe*). A villain once merely lived on a farm in Roman times ; he was to become a serf and, finally, a bad man. This kind of social prejudice is matched by xeno-phobia or hatred or contempt of the foreign, making the Portuguese for ' word '—*palavra*—into ' palaver '. As the *hoc est corpus* of the Mass has become ' hocus pocus ', so Mary Magdalene's weeping has become ' maudlin ', and the fairings from St Audrey's fair ' tawdry '. Ameliora-tive changes—in which the worse becomes the better—are far rarer than pejorative ones : one should note ' nice ', though—*nescius* (' igno-rant ') in Latin, and always unfavourable (it could mean either ' lasci-vious ' or ' trivial ') in Shakespeare's time.

It is interesting to see what we do with foreign importations in our own day. The *Blitz* of *Blitzkrieg* lost its native meaning of ' lightning ' and now carries connotations of wanton destruction and massive bravery. ' Beatnik '—a hybrid of American-Jewish origin—meant a member of a group devoted to pacifism and self-denial but has quickly become as contemptuous a term as ' teddy-boy ' (itself an example of pejorative change). Conversely, ' spiv '—which had a brief currency just after the war with a cluster of bad meanings—was taken over by the French as an adjective : *très spiv,* as applied to a garment, meant ' stylish '—a good example of ameliorative change. The Malay word *pĕrang,* meaning ' war ', passed into RAF usage with the particularised meaning of an attack, usually a ' wizard ' one. Other, more recent, borrowings, like *sputnik, espresso,* have kept close to the things originally described ; *ombudsman,* like science fiction, provides us with the name before the referent.

English is quick to develop old words to serve new purposes. Often *apocope* is the way (cutting off the body but retaining the head), as in ' pop ' (' popular music '), ' trad ' (' traditional jazz '). ' Television ' quickly became ' telly '—a half-contemptuous, half-affectionate shortening. One of the simplest and most telling of adaptations has been in the field of rocketry, where ' go ' is now an adjective meaning ' fully prepared '. The age of brinkmanship and the nymphet is quick to satisfy its semantic needs ; it is even looking ahead, in its masochistic way, with the term ' megadeath '. Let us hope its referent stays in the world of real, not metaphorical, nightmare.

NINE

SENTENCES

A WORD in a dictionary is very much like a car in a mammoth motor-show—full of potential but temporarily inactive. To get the car on the road a whole complex of things is required—fuel and a controller at the wheel, direction and traffic-signs. To get a word moving we need the things that come under the heading of *grammar*. Grammar is a technique for describing words in action. It classifies words into parts of speech, lists the changes of form that words can undergo when in contact with other words (*accidence*), examines the placing of the totality of words needed for the expression of thought into a significant order or pattern (*syntax*).

Because grammar looks like a science and yet does not behave like one (words often jump out of their classificatory cages), teachers and textbook-writers have been wary of delving too deeply into it. A lot of out-of-date conceptions lie fossilised in grammar-books, and their makers—who often have stockbroker incomes—do not like to admit this. Nor does the inertia of teachers or the examiner's love of the unambiguous encourage them to revise the thirty-third edition. It is best to let things carry on as they are ; let sleeping dogmas lie. The pupil-examinees do not want fresh light on grammar ; they merely want to get rid of it.

Grammarians like the one whose funeral Browning describes first made their appearance at the time of the New Learning. They wanted to analyse the linguistic data offered by Greek and Latin (a grammar school is strictly speaking a Latin grammar school) ; inevitably, when they turned to describe the behaviour of the vernacular they took their classical grammatical apparatus with them. Most of the languages of Europe have, ever since, been analysed as though they *ought* to be the tongue of Homer or Horace. Some grammarians have smacked the bottom of English because it has carelessly lost all its genders and most of its case-endings. This is not cricket, meaning not Latin. Fortunately for them, few European grammarians have ever been called upon to examine a non-Aryan language like Chinese or Tibetan and equip it with a descriptive apparatus. The fact is that English, German, French, and the rest will, to some extent, yield to the categories of Latin because, like Latin, they are Aryan or Indo-European languages. But Japanese and Eskimo, not having had a classical upbringing, refuse to play the game.

The smugness of scholars like John Stuart Mill, who saw in the 'eight parts of speech' fundamental categories of human thought, required, and still requires, the cold douche of contact with an Asiatic language. There is nothing universal about our Western grammatical compartments, and, at best, they are somewhat shoddy and makeshift even when applied to the languages for which they were formulated. There are too many assumptions, too little desire (there never is much where vested interests are involved) to look facts in the face.

One assumption is that every sentence (meaning every complete statement) has to have a subject and a predicate, meaning at least one noun and one verb, as in 'Dad drinks' or 'Mum nags'. Grammarians know that many complete statements (statements made complete by context of situation) do not fulfil this fundamental law. The following are in common use and hence are good English: 'Fire!'—'Out of it!'—'Away!'—'Oh, no!'—'Go!'—'Help!' Grammar insists that, in a ghostly sort of way, the parts of speech required to make a full subject-and-predicate form are really there but have been suppressed: they are 'understood'. They re-formulate these utterances as follows: '(There is a) fire!'—'(You get) out of it!'—'(Go) away!'—'Oh, no, (don't do it/I'm not having that/I disagree/etc.)'—'(You) go!'—'(Somebody) help (me)!'

The falseness of these assumptions should be self-evident: at no level of the brain does the speaker of the so-called 'elliptical' utterances imagine the 'understood' words. But the grammarian may point to some earlier stage of the language, when the understood forms, now suppressed, were fully expressed. His whole argument falls down when we see that languages have always used the device of a single-word utterance, that the missing forms only exist in the grammarian's mind. We are right to remind him that his job is to examine and analyse the forms of speech in actual use –what is, not what should be.

A further exploding of the Western theory that a verb is an essential part of a sentence is contrived through an examination of languages like

Russian, Chinese, and Malay, which have never possessed the *copula*—
the verb ' to be ', as in sentences like ' He is a good man '. Malay
renders this as ' *Dia* (he) *orang* (man) *baik* (good) ' and Russian as ' *On*
(he)—*dobriy* (good) *chelovyek* (man) '. There is no point in the Western
grammarian's asserting that ' is ' must be understood ; how can a word
be understood if it does not even exist as a part of speech ?

We must, then, revise our views as to what a sentence is, particularly
rejecting the subterfuge of ' ellipsis ' and the ' understood ' subject or
predicate. English has never felt any sense of the unnatural in its
omission of verbs. Newspaper headlines miss them out consistently
and, in doing so, merely seem to be exploiting a natural English tendency—enshrined historically in ' Up, guards, and at 'em ' and
proverbially in ' Red sky at night, shepherd's delight ', ' More haste,
less speed ', ' The more the merrier ', and so on.

To see what categories of speech the grammarian considers important,
we ought to make up some typically ' grammar-book ' sentences (that
is, sentences that do not give the Latinist palpitations) and examine
the function of the words therein.

(*a*) THE GIRL IS PRETTY. (SHE IS PRETTY.)

' Girl ' is a noun, subject of the verb ' is '. For ' girl ' ' she ' can be
substituted ; this makes ' she ' a pronoun. ' The ' is a bound form
which cannot be categorised except as the definite article. Attempts to
describe it as an adjective cannot really be justified. ' Pretty ' is an
adjective (it qualifies the noun if placed close to it ; it is predicated
of the noun if it comes after ' is ') and its behaviour is manifestly
different from that of ' the '. ' Girls are pretty ' makes sense ; ' Girls
are the ' does not. ' Is ' is a verb of a special kind. As, like ' seems ' and
' becomes ', it cannot express total meaning in itself (unless used
theologically or metaphysically), it can be called a *synsemantic verb*.
' Be ! ' makes no sense, nor does ' Become ! ' or ' Seem ! ', but ' Glow ! '
or ' Go ! ' or ' Come ! ' makes sense enough : words like the latter can
be called *autosemantic verbs*.

(*b*) THIS PRETTY GIRL SHALL BE MY WIFE.
　　THE GIRL WITH THE FLAXEN HAIR SHALL BE MY WIFE.
　　THAT GIRL, WHOM I HAVE ADORED EVER SINCE MY EARLY MANHOOD,
　　　SHALL BE MY WIFE.

These three sentences are identical in their essential structure—

'—Girl shall be my wife'. In the first sentence we see 'this'—a demonstrative adjective, in the third sentence 'that'—again a demonstrative adjective. The phrase 'with the flaxen hair' in the second sentence is doing the same sort of work as 'pretty' in the first. If 'pretty' is an adjective, 'with the flaxen hair' can be called an adjective phrase (or word-group). Phrases of this kind tend to begin with a preposition (a particle expressing relationship between the noun which is subject or object of a verb and the noun which is the core of the phrase) :

> THE GIRL with the flaxen hair
> on the bus
> in my dreams
> from East Sussex
> at the house on the corner

In the third sentence, the word-group 'whom I have adored ever since my early manhood' is doing an adjectival job (it is interchangeable with the adjective 'adorable', for example). It is not quite an adjective phrase, for it contains two pure sentence elements—'I' and 'have adored' (a subject and a verb) ; we call it an adjective clause. Such clauses begin with a relative pronoun—a word that refers back to a word in the main sentence (in this case, 'girl') and at the same time links this main sentence (in this case, 'That girl shall be my wife') to the adjective clause itself. Here are other examples of adjective clauses :

> THE GIRL whom I see every day on the bus
> who lives next door
> whose mother works in my office
> with whom I play tennis OR
> whom I play tennis with OR
> I play tennis with

This last adjective clause is genuinely elliptical : 'whom' is really understood. This omission of a relative pronoun is rare in other languages.

(c) HE WILL COME TONIGHT.
> HE WILL COME AT ABOUT QUARTER PAST NINE.
> HE WILL COME WHEN THE SUN IS SETTING.

In the first sentence, 'tonight' tells us more about the proposed action expressed in the verb ' will come '. ' Tonight ' is therefore an adverb. ' At about quarter past nine ' (note the preposition at the beginning) is an adverb phrase. ' When the sun is setting ' (or ' As soon as the sun sets ' or ' While the sun is going down ') contains a subject-predicate combination (' sun/sets '). The introductory word or phrase (' when ' or ' while ' or ' as soon as ') joins the two sentences ' He will come ' and ' when/while/as soon as the sun etc.' It is thus a join-word or conjunction, like ' and ' or ' but ' or ' also '. The adverb ' tonight ' and the two adverb-substitutes express time (they answer the question ' When will he come ? ') but a number of other adverbial notions can be expressed :

MANNER :   COME quickly
           with all haste
           as if your life depended on it

PLACE :   WAIT here
           by the old mill-stream
           where the three roads meet

REASON :   Why (do) I DO IT ?
                for kicks
                because I like it

CONCESSION :   Nevertheless   HE IS UNHAPPY
           Despite his wealth
           Although he is rich

We must note that adverbs of manner—' quickly ', ' beautifully '— and adverbs of degree—' more ', ' most ', ' rather '—can modify an adjective (' beautifully warm ' ; ' most kind ') or an adverb (' exceptionally badly ' ; ' rather coldly '). Whether we are right to call them adverbs when they are really adjective-helpers or adverb-helpers is a matter for discussion, especially when a word like ' very ' cannot modify a verb.

(d) I like   WOMEN   don't like me
    I like   TO DANCE   is to know the poetry of motion
    I like   WALKING IN THE FIELDS   is good exercise
    I like   WHAT YOU DID THEN   was uncalled-for.

The forms in capitals can act as object of ' I like ' or as subject of what comes after. ' Women ' is a noun ; ' to dance ' is a noun phrase (infinitive form : verb without subject preceded by the preposition ' to ') ; ' walking ' is a verbal noun followed by a phrase which sits on the borderline between an adjective phrase (what sort of walking ?) and an adverb phrase (where is the walking ?) The final noun-substitute is a noun clause : note the subject-predicate ' you/did ' preceded by the relative pronoun ' What '.

There is no room here for a fuller account of the parts of speech we recognise in English sentences. We ought to add that the odd interpolated forms like ' Of course ', ' not likely ', ' most emphatically not ', ' with all my heart ', as well as plain ' yes ' and ' no ' can be called affirmative and negative words and phrases, while expressions like ' Er . . .', ' Well . . .', ' you see . . .' can best be regarded as punctuation forms which break up the flow of a statement without contributing much to the meaning. These ' thrown-in ' words and phrases are often assigned to a rag-bag category called the *Interjection*, created to accommodate otherwise unclassifiable elements. Some of history's great cries of agony, like ' My Son, my son ! ' or ' Light, light ! ' or Faustus's ' Ah, Mephistophiles . . .' are, to the strict old-time grammarian, not really analysable as complete utterances. They have been regarded as mere ' throw-ins ', not sentences at all. So much the worse for the strict old-time grammarian.

Terms like ' noun ', ' adjective ', ' verb ', and so on are useful generalising tools which help us to cope with the problems of learning foreign languages. We can learn a good deal from a table like this :

Adjective before Noun	Noun before Adjective
English	French (normally)
German	Spanish
Russian	Malay
Chinese	Welsh
French, when adjective is not really precise (*beau garçon ; bonne idée*, etc.)	

There is a disconcerting logic about German which, putting the adjective before the noun, puts the whole of an adjective phrase there, too. English has ' buttered bread ' but ' bread spread with butter and strawberry jam ' ; German has ' with butter and strawberry jam spread bread '. In other words, in speaking German, one must have the entire content of one's adjective phrase worked out before the noun which it qualifies makes its appearance. This to some extent applies also to noun, adjective, and adverb clauses, for in these the verb is always shunted to the end. A sentence like ' This is the girl with whom I to the cinema went ' calls for precise formulation of the clause before utterance, so does 'He told me that I forgiven was'. Note this separation of the subject from the verb, seen at its most idiosyncratic with a compound verb like ' I shall have gone '. This consists of (a) subject ' I ' ; (b) *finite* (i.e. subject-taking part of verb) ' shall ' ; (c) infinitive ' have ' ; (d) past participle ' gone '. In a German noun clause the English order is reversed : ' He told me that by that time I gone have shall '—in other words, giving the formula (a) (d) (c) (b). Similarly, one has ' I think that he it done have must '. One ought to practise such seeming perversions in English before trying them out in German. Even in ordinary sentences, German prefers to have a compound verb curiously split up : ' I have to him spoken ' ; ' He has it arranged.' This is analogous to out-moded English poetic forms like ' Him have I often seen, with torso bare ', where English also takes on the adjective-position of the Romance languages.

There are two aspects of grammar which cause heart-burnings when languages of a conservative type—like German or Russian—or old languages like Latin and Greek have to be learned. These are (a) a rich system of *inflections*, whereby a noun or verb changes its ending according to the job it is doing in the sentence and (b) a complete panoply of *genders*, so that some nouns are masculine, some feminine, others neuter. More progressive languages, like English, have discarded gender and most of the noun inflections, while Italian and Spanish, retaining all the wealth of verb-endings bequeathed by Latin, have simplified the noun and made gender no real problem. Persian, Malay, and Chinese have no gender and no inflections : through studying these languages we learn how much useless luggage the grammar-books of the progressive West have still to carry.

Gender, in fact, is a luxury which contributes nothing to meaning. If I say *le bière* and *la café* I am breaking fundamental French rules but not rendering myself unintelligible. In English, where gender only persists with sea-going craft, it may be a breach of etiquette to call a ship ' it ' and not ' she ', but no semantic law is transgressed against. It may seem wasteful that English needs ' he ' and ' she ' essentially only for human beings, while ' it ' has to embrace everything else, but English has at least resolved the old confusion between sex and gender, which need not have anything to do with each other at all. In German *das Mädchen* is neuter, though it means ' the young girl ', and ' the horse '—*das Pferd*—is also neuter, whether gelded or not. In Russian ' dog ' (*sobaka*) is feminine even when male, and Latin *poeta* (' poet ') belongs to a feminine declension. It has been suggested that gender had its origins in animism—that primitive attitude to nature which gave everything a soul and saw biological sex as a necessary attribute of the animate. It is more likely that gender is an attempt—at a later stage of human development—to impose order on disorder, to herd a mass of primitive particulars into a few general groups, using the sexual categories—of which ' neuter', which posits the *absence* of sex, is logically one—as the best known and most convenient. Such categories have also been applied to metals, and dies, screws, and templates are still given a ' male ' or ' female ' appellation. With ' bastard ' files the whole sexual business is taken even further.

The only motive for categorising nouns according to gender—which means according to *ending*—is a syntactical one : gender is important only if other words (not nouns) are affected by it. In Latin, *murus* (' wall ') is masculine, *porta* (' door ') is feminine, and *tectum* (' roof ') is neuter. This involves a particular choice when we want to apply the adjective ' good ' to these words. *Murus* must be *bonus*, *porta* must be *bona*, *tectum* must be *bonum*. Words are fond of influencing each other in this way. Old English had a full set of genders in nouns and corresponding endings in adjectives ; these have only disappeared in Modern English because, with phonological change, the endings that indicated gender have dropped off : *mona* has become ' moon ', *ealu* has become ' ale ', *sunu* has become ' sun ' and so on. In the daughters of Latin the gender principle has declined : the masculine nouns of Latin remain masculine, the feminine have remained feminine, but the Latin neuters have been adopted by the masculine gender : thus, *tectum* has become *le toit* in French, *il tetto* in Italian, *el techo* in Spanish.

The definite article in the modern Romance (or Latin) languages is derived from the Latin demonstratives *ille* and *illa*—the masculine and feminine forms respectively for ' that ' (the English ' the ' has a similar derivation from the Anglo-Saxon demonstrative). All of them agree on *la* for the feminine article ; *le, il, el* represent different decisions as to what to make out of *ille*. The indefinite article (*un/une ; un/una*) has been made out of the Latin numerical adjective *unus -a -um*, meaning 'one'. Gender, then, determines the choice of a word for 'the'. (In German we have three to choose from—*der/die/das*.) It also tells us—as in Latin—what adjectival ending to choose—simple enough in the Romance tongues but difficult in German, where the adjectival ending will vary according to whether the definite or indefinite article (as well as other genuine demonstratives) or no article at all comes before. In Russian, the verb-ending in the past tense depends on the gender of the subject—as though English had 'John slept' but 'Mary slepta'.

Gender-learning is a nuisance to us because of our complete emancipation from it in our own language. It does not matter to us when we are reading a foreign language, so long as that language has a clearly defined word-order, so that we know which adjective qualifies which noun. But in Latin, where word-order is fluid, especially in poetry, agreement between noun and adjective may be our only way of making sense out of a passage. In learning to speak enough of a modern foreign language to find our way about, we need not take gender too seriously if it causes us genuine distress. There are some varieties of German where *der*, *die*, *das* are blurred and slurred into a sort of omnibus *de* and adjectival endings are similarly indistinct. Even if our genders are all wrong—and this applies to any language—we can still be understood, for in modern languages gender is not *functional*—it is a mere decorative survival of any earlier stage of the language. For a language teacher to spend his first lessons concentrating on gender with a class that cannot see the use of it—this is near-criminal.

Accidence is mainly concerned with examining patterns of word-endings as they appear in that total meaningful structure we call a sentence. Nouns in Latin are very fully 'inflected' : a noun will vary its ending according to its relationship with other words. *Mensa* is a 'table' (the English 'mess' in its military sense is ultimately derived from it), but only if it is the subject of a verb : *Mensa* is here. For the rest, I kick the *mensam*, admire the colour (of the) *mensae*, give a good polish (to the) *mensae*, take a leg from the *mensā*. There can be many *mensae* in a shop, and we can admire all these *mensas*. The colours (of the) *mensarum* can be admirable, and we would like to walk off with all the *mensis*. This seems complicated and confusing, but it is only a matter of using a glued-on ending instead of a free preposition. If English glued its prepositions on to the end of ' table ', instead of having them in front of the word, we would have something like this :

Singular		Plural
table	*Nominative*	tables
table	*Accusative*	tables
tableof	*Genitive*	tablesof
tableto	*Dative*	tablesto
tableby,	*Ablative*	tablesby,
tablewith, or		tableswith, or
tablefrom		tablesfrom

The noun in English used to have a whole set of such *cases*, and modern German still uses them. Here is the word for ' day ' in Anglo-Saxon and German (masculine in both languages) :

ANGLO-SAXON

	Nom.	*Acc.*	*Gen.*	*Dat.*
Singular	daeg	daeg	daeges	daege
Plural	dagas	dagas	daga	dagum

GERMAN

Singular	Tag	Tag	Tages	Tage
Plural	Tage	Tage	Tage	Tagen
	Nom.	*Acc.*	*Gen.*	*Dat.*

The genitive singular survives in English, always acceptable for nouns denoting living things—like ' John's ', ' boy's', 'girl's', 'dog's'—though ' 's ' strictly turns a noun into an adjective (the apostrophe, incidentally, manifestly commemorates a departed ' e ', though Elizabethan etymologists saw there a truncated form of ' his '). We are not too happy about expressions like ' the apple's core ', ' the door's handle ', ' the box's lid ', though one cannot say that they are ' wrong '. By a simple act of extension, an ' s ' sign of possession is also used in plurals : ' women's '; ' men's '; ' mothers' '; ' boys' '.

The Romance languages have dropped all noun inflections except for a plural indicator. This is straightforward in Spanish, where an ' s ' is invariably used, and straightforward enough in French, where ' s ' (*homme/hommes*) or ' x ' (*bureau/bureaux*) is very often a purely visual

sign. Here the plural article is the true indicator of a plural : *l'homme* =
/lɔm/ ; *les hommes* = /lezɔm/. Italian plurals tend to follow the Latin
pattern, changing ' o ' to ' i ' and ' a ' to ' e ' (*ragazzo/ragazzi ; donna/
donne*). English, so progressive in other ways, uses a very mixed bag.
' S '—indicating /s/ or /z/—we may regard as the regular pluraliser,
but forms like ' ox/oxen ', ' child/children ', ' brother/brethren '
represent an older and very Teutonic way of making plurals, as do
' man/men ', ' ' woman/women ' (/wʊmən/wɪmɪn/), ' mouse/mice ',
' tooth/teeth ', ' goose/geese ', and so on. This latter kind of plural
is to be found in Anglo-Saxon, and it seems to suggest some earlier -i
ending which acted on the main vowel and (/i/ being a front vowel)
dragged it towards the front of the mouth. If we imagine that something
like /mus/ (' mouse ') was pluralised as /musi/, then it seems reasonable
for the /u/ to be brought forward to /y/ (the sound in *lune*), remaining
there even after the pluralising -i had dropped off. This kind of
assimilation (one sound influencing another) is common in the Teutonic
languages, of which English is one. The plural of Anglo-Saxon *mūs* was,
in fact, *mys*, and the /yː/ in the plural has become unrounded. The
/miˑs/—' meece '—which a TV cartoon cat still favours—became /maɪs/
in the ordinary course of the vowel-shifts we have already discussed.

Children and comic songs (' Ours is a nice house, ours is : we've got
no rats nor mouses ') rationalise English plurals, and the few eccentric-
seeming ones we have either fascinate foreigners (who delight in the
' child/children ' pattern) or are easily avoided by them (I have an
English-writing Russian correspondent who prefers to tell me about his
' kids '). German, however, is happier with this mutation of vowels
on the ' man/men ' principle than with any other of the pluralising
devices available, and plurals like the following are regular and normal :
*Bach/Bäch ; Bogen/Bögen ; Chor/Chöre ; Drang/Dränge ; Genuss/
Genüsse*. The two dots are merely a ' fronting ' signal.

Personal pronouns remain complicated in most Western languages,
and they show a strange lack of willingness to ' generalise ' which must
be traced back to the unknown tongue which was the mother of the
Indo-Germanic group. Thus ' I ' bears no resemblance to ' me ' in
English, nor *Jeg* to *mig* in Icelandic, not *Ya* to *mne* in Russian, nor *ego*
to *me* in Latin. We see the same lack of sound-pattern in ' we '/' us ',
Russian *mi/nas*, German *wir/uns*, Icelandic *vjer/oss*. This is no law of
linguistic nature, for Malay has *saya* and Chinese has *wo* as an invariable

I-me form. English has tried to simplify its personal pronouns over the centuries, though earlier forms survive in dialect and colloquial speech. ' Bash 'em,' ' Give 'em hell ' contain an abbreviated form of the old ' hem ' (not ' them '), and the rural ' Tell un ' (' Tell him ') goes back to ' hine '. The Lancashire word for ' she ' is ' oo ' (/ɯː/), which is a survival of Anglo-Saxon ' heo ', abandoned in favour of the demonstrative ' sio ', whence ' she '.

English now recognises only two inflections for all pronouns—the subjective (or nominative) ' I ', ' you ', ' we ', ' he ', ' she ', ' they ', and the objective (or accusative) ' me ', ' you ', ' him ', ' her ', ' them ', ' us '. The objective form is used after transitive verbs like ' love ', ' hit ', ' kick ', and also after prepositions like ' after ', ' between ', ' for '. It is because ' you ' has become an invariable form—both in case and in number—that the solecisms ' Between you and I ' and ' Let you and I ' are committed. It is through the operation of such analogies (if ' you ' can be invariable, why not ' I ' as well ?) that languages can be simplified.

The greatest richness of inflection is to be found in the verbs of the Indo-Germanic languages, such richness seeming just and necessary if we remember that the verbs of the older tongues, like Latin, were not helped by personal pronouns. If we pervert an English verb, as we perverted an English noun, glueing the pronouns on to the end, we can see that the corresponding Latin verb is not so unreasonable after all :

English	*Latin*
loveI	amo
lovestthou	amas
loveshe, lovesshe, lovesit	amat
lovewe	amamus
loveyou	amatis
lovethey	amant

The tendency in the Germanic languages has been for the inflections of the verb to become simplified, leaving the work of person-indication to pronouns, so that the great majority of English verbs may some day follow the example of ' must ', discarding even the ' -s ' of the third person (' he love ' ; ' she eat ' ; ' it bark ').

Latin grammarians (meaning the classifying men of the Renaissance) never found it so easy to categorise verbs as to categorise nouns. This is why students of Latin have so many pages of principal parts of irregular verbs to learn by heart, some of them—like *fero, ferre, tuli, latum*—so fantastically irregular as never to be forgotten. The insistence on setting irregular verbs to be learnt is often misguided : it sets sheer form above meaning and forgets that one may go through life without having to use—or even to recognise in speech or literature— the more irregular of the irregulars. One may go quite a long way in French with the auxiliaries *être* and *avoir* and the verbs of the so-called first conjugation (those whose infinitives end in *-er*). The beginner in English can subsist equally well on the ' weak verbs ' (eked out with ' to be ', ' to have ', ' to go ') until he is sufficiently familiar with the ' feel ' of the language not to be scared by irregularities.

' To understand all is to forgive all.' We have invoked this maxim in connection with the seeming illogicalities of English spelling. We can invoke it also with, say, ' go ' and ' went ', which do not seem to be part of the same verb at all and, indeed, are not. ' Go ' is defective in that it lacks a past tense and has to borrow the past tense of ' wend ' (' I wend my way ' ; ' I went my way '.) We see ' I sing ' ; ' I sang ' ; ' I have sung ' (a ' strong verb ') and wonder how it can inhabit the same linguistic world as ' I chant ' ; ' I chanted ' ; ' I have chanted ' (a ' weak verb '). The fact is that all languages like to conserve, hate to discard, and the strong form belongs to an early stage of development while the weak one belongs to a later—and apparently more amenable—stage, and both subsist, cheek by jowl, in the same vocabulary. Only by creating artificial languages like Esperanto or Novial can we hope to achieve perfect logic and perfect regularity, and then we soon become sated with the mechanical deadness of perfection, longing for something more human and less regular—the ' madness ' of Russian grammar, the waywardness of English orthography.

Grammar has its own fascination and, in a mystical way, its own peculiar truth. We may not know what the verb ' grobble ' means, but we can be pretty sure that if I grobble, he grobbles and that, some time in the past, we both grobbled together. If ' grobble ' is a noun, then 1 grobble + 1 grobble = 2 grobbles. There is a satisfactory *boniness* about grammar which the flesh of sheer vocabulary requires before it can become vertebrate and walk the earth. But to study it for its own sake, without relating it to function, is utter madness.

PART TWO

LANGUAGES IN PARTICULAR

ONE

LEARNING FOREIGN LANGUAGES

1

THE English, in their splendid isolation, used to regard foreigners as either a comic turn or a sexual menace. To learn a European language (other than the dead ones from which English had kindly borrowed) was, at best, to seek to acquire a sort of girl's-finishing-school ornament, at worst, to capitulate weakly to the enemy. Things are not very different now, but an uneasy awareness is dawning that linguistic isolation is no longer possible, that the tongues of these damned Europeans may have to be taken seriously if they persist in pretending not to understand English. Unfortunately, many educated Europeans *do* understand English and are very ready to speak it to English travellers and write it to English business firms, thus soothing that uneasy awareness back into island complacency. But, in their soberest moments, most English people will admit that the attitude of ' Let them learn our language, blast them ' will no longer do.

The ability to speak three or four foreign languages with moderate proficiency is looked on still with suspicion by English people of an insular bent. But by most it is grudgingly admitted to be clever, even a mark of genius. And yet many Welshmen carry their bilingualism very lightly ; Swiss citizens know French, German, often Italian, as well as what they learn at school ; a Chinese bar-boy in Malaya can cope with Malay, English, and often two or three dialects of Chinese ; a Port Said dragoman will know at least ten languages (I met one who knew fifteen, as well as three English dialects). People like this are not towering intellectuals ; they are people often of very moderate intelligence. What makes them good at languages is the fact that economic and social circumstances force them to be good. So far, the people of England have never really been forced out of their monoglot complacency, and the legend that there is something in the Englishman's genes that prevents his becoming proficient in languages continues to be fostered.

And yet English colonial administrators, as well as planters, have not merely mastered the languages of Africa and the East but given them dictionaries, grammars, even literatures. In any crowded public bar it will not be hard to find at least one man who can understand demotic Arabic, Urdu, or Malay. If a good enough motive can be adduced (soldier's hunger or loneliness, the colonial officer's proficiency bar), then a foreign language will be learned, and learned thoroughly. To find as urgent a motive in peace-time and at home is more difficult ; the mood of exile is one thing, the cosy tiredness of after-work evening— the daily paper and the television beckoning—quite another.

I have in mind, of course, the learning of foreign languages as an adult undertaking, a matter of choice. Let us look first, however, at the reasons put forward for the learning of foreign languages in schools, where choice is hardly involved at all. In the grammar and public schools there seems to be no unification of motive behind the teaching of ancient and the teaching of modern languages. Latin and Greek are the tongues of two civilisations which have helped to make our own, therefore they must be accorded a peculiar reverence ; learning them is an excellent mental discipline ; they are logical and lucid and help us to write English well ; they enshrine important literatures. These are the reasons put forward for their continuing high place in the curriculum, and—except for the last—they are not very convincing reasons. Ancient languages, with their batteries of irregularities, are far less logical than modern Chinese ; only the study of English can help us to write English. On the other hand, there is a peculiar aesthetic thrill to be gained from reading Latin or Greek poets in the original, and this may well be the only justification for learning the languages : poetry, as Dr Johnson said, is untranslatable and hence, if it is good, it preserves the language it is written in. But to read Caesar's accounts of his conquests or Pliny on the habits of dolphins, one does not really need any Latin : a good modern translation will suffice. Herodotus, similarly, can be read with fair confidence in English, but the peculiar music of Sophocles cannot be rendered into any modern tongue—not even modern Greek.

The suggestion that secondary schools should teach only enough Latin and Greek (both languages ; not just one) to enable a boy or girl to read Vergil and Homer with a crib will be regarded in many quarters as an heretical one. I make it seriously, however. The virtues of knowing how to write a good Latin or Greek composition are, surely, chimerical ; unseen translation is of the same highbrow cross-word-puzzle order. We shculd only translate English into Latin for the benefit of a Roman, but all the Romans are long dead. If a ' key ' will help us to work out the meaning of a Latin or Greek passage, why should we not use a key ? There will always be classical scholars who will need more than the minimal training I suggest—editors of texts and makers of keys—but for the greater number it should be enough to be given a fairly painless entrée into the beauties of classical poetry and drama, the preservation of which is the only purpose behind preserving the languages they are written in.

We learn Latin not to juggle with subjunctives and gerunds but to get at the Roman spirit—that ' pagan night ', for instance, which we find superbly expressed in Catullus and which had such a radical influence on our own seventeenth-century poets :

> *Soles occidere et redire possunt :*
> *Nobis cum semel occidit brevis lux,*
> *Nox est perpetua una dormienda.*
> *Da mihi basia mille, deinde centum,*
> *Dein mille altera, dein secunda centum,*
> *Deinde usque altera mille, deinde centum . . .*

A literal translation and a minimum of linguistic exposition should enable a teacher to give even a person with no Latin at all some notion of the meaning of this passage. Here, first, is a line-by-line translation :

> Suns can (may) set and return :
> For us, when once the short light has set,
> There is one perpetual night to-be-slept-through.
> Give me a thousand kisses, then a hundred,
> Then another thousand, then a second hundred,
> Then yet another thousand, then a hundred . . .

Following traditional learning methods, no student of Latin could expect to approach a passage like this until the slow toil of learning paradigms and parts of irregular verbs had been completed. I see no reason why linguistic exposition of the passage should not follow a more empirical line—the breaking-up of words into their constituent morphemes. Thus, *sol-* means ' sun ' (compare English ' solar ', ' solstice ') ;

-es is a pluralising morpheme corresponding to English *-s*. *Occide-* means ' set ' (of the sun), and it is to be found in the word ' occidental ' (' western ') ; *-re* is an infinitive ending found also at the end of *redire*. *Poss-* has the root meaning found in the English derivative ' possible '. Of verb-endings found in this passage, *-t* always stands for third person singular (he, she, it), while *-nt* signifies third person plural (they). *Da* means ' give ', the *-a* carrying an imperative force.

Apart from the characteristic morphemes of Latin which indicate the behaviour of the words, a good deal of the vocabulary of Catullus's poem is already possessed by the English student who knows no Latin at all. Even *basia* (' kisses ')—though no English derivative exists— may be known from Spanish popular songs like *Besame* (' Kiss me ') or *Eso beso* (' That kiss '). If *dein* and *deinde* (both meaning ' then ') seem to denote an inconsistency, one must remember that this is a poem and that a certain poetic licence is admissible. But even in non-poetic English we use ' till ' and ' until ' indifferently.

The point about selecting a passage of verse or prose which shall give aesthetic pleasure, and then submitting it to linguistic analysis, is precisely that the end of learning a language can be presented along with the process of learning. In studying grammar, we swim miserably in a marmoreal sea of abstractions, wondering at the point of it all. In reading—however haltingly—even a very few lines of a Roman poet, we do not wonder : the point is there before us.

2

THE purpose of teaching modern foreign languages is usually presented as primarily utilitarian : we want to converse with Frenchmen or Germans, to read their newspapers, understand their films, write and receive letters in their languages ; it is also conceded that we may want to get to know their literatures. These aims are sound but rarely fulfilled. The tripper to Paris will find Paris only too happy to sell him everything in English, including the English newspapers ; also he will find a minimum of pen-pals. Let us be honest and admit that few English people need foreign languages for the well-beaten holiday paths. In any case, one does not want to limit one's travelling to those countries which speak the languages one learned at school.

The final argument for learning the ancient languages is one of the most compelling for learning the modern languages as well—namely, that certain literary pleasures are unavailable in translation. The educated man, it is generally felt, should be able to read Racine, Goethe, Dante, Lorca—with, anyway, the aid of a crib. To know these only in translation is not to know them at all. And even prose literature (since the Renaissance, that is) does not yield all its magic in translation: Edmund Wilson has recently told us that we had better not deliver any literary judgement on *Doctor Zhivago* until we have come into contact with its word-play and symbolism, which are, inevitably, confined to the original. One feels uneasy at reading Proust or Flaubert in translation, despite the excellent English versions that exist. The ultimate value of a translation lies in its power to ease our way into the original.

It would seem, then, that our formal educations should equip us with at least a reading knowledge of those major European languages that do not find their way into the curriculum for specialist treatment. 'Modern Languages' in most schools means French and German, mainly because there are so many French and German specialists available. But there are increasing signs that other Romance languages are finding their way in, as also Slavonic languages. One of the incontestable advantages of the Comprehensive School is the opportunity it grants for almost limitless choice in the linguistic field—in theory, anyway: we have still far too few teachers of Oriental languages and far too many teachers of French.

Any school should be able to offer, in addition to specialist courses in Modern Languages, a supplementary (or even alternative) course in Linguistic Elements, in which the bases of General Phonetics could be started in the first year (the eleven-plus year, that is), gentle comparative work on the Romance languages could follow in the second year, and reading German—and even Russian—could be added in successive years. One could envisage a pleasant GCE (O Level) paper on General Language, in which questions like the following could be asked:

(1) Describe the organic processes involved in uttering the word ' thing '.

(2) Render your own pronunciation of the following into phonetic (IPA) script:

' Time and the hour run through the roughest day.'

E

(3) Break the following down into its constituent morphemes, describing the function of each :
   ' John's sister was unwilling to provide him with any financial assistance.'

(4) Transcribe the following phonetically :
   fille (French) ; *figlia* (Italian) ; *filha* (Portuguese) ; *hija* (Spanish) Describe briefly the adventures that the Latin word *filia* has undergone in changing into these four words.

(5) German *Zahn* and English *tooth* are cognate with the Gothic *tunthus*. What processes of historical change do you think the German and English words have undergone since the time when they both resembled *tunthus* ?

(6) Write down the following names in (*a*) Arabic (*b*) Cyrillic (*c*) Greek script :
   Johnson ; Khrushchev ; Douglas-Home ; New York ; Washington.

(7) Free translation of a passage from a French, Italian, Spanish, or German newspaper.

3

OUR main purpose here is to ease the task of language-learning for the average adult. It is sadly true that we only begin to feel the urgent need to learn a foreign language when we have left school. The need may be commercial or social, or it may be an itch of sheer curiosity (it is often this last that produces the amateur student of Tibetan or Basque). Granted the need and the staying power, we can either enrol in part-time classes or—with the aid of books and records—teach ourselves at home. Firmness of motive is very important ; any teacher of evening classes will know that those of his students who have no real reason for learning Spanish but ' thought it might be something useful to do in the winter evenings ' will not last beyond the third or fourth lesson at most. The same thing can happen with the home learner : the books on French are not so immediately interesting as the latest Agatha Christie ; the records of *Russian Self-Taught* are less soothing than a Frank Sinatra LP ; one is tired ; one has no gift for languages after all ; everybody in Gambogia speaks English. The voices of these devils can only be stilled by a sense of the fundamental importance of what we are trying to do, and also by a technique which makes the process of learning interesting in itself.

Unfortunately, most of the primers on modern languages available to the home student are, where easy to follow, amateurish and, where professional, discouraging. Some primers still inhabit a dream-world where the words for ' international co-operation ' are available but the words for ' yes ' and ' no ' hard to find. My own language library has a book on Finnish which gives neither ' please ' nor ' thank you ', a Russian primer which tells of a maggot in a cherry but not the lack of toilet-paper in the toilet, a work on colloquial Arabic which is a miracle of scholarship but a daunting guide to the simple mechanics of touristic need. When buying a foreign language primer, look first at the guide to pronunciation, see if the author has any real phonetic knowledge ; then examine the range of vocabulary, see if the important things (drink, aspirins, bus-stops, traveller's cheques) take precedence over the modern equivalent of lightning-struck postillions ; finally, see whether grammar is rejoiced in as an end in itself or treated as a minimal skeleton to the flesh of speech. You will, alas, find very few books which are really satisfactory. You will end, as I normally end, by gutting the book you have bought and using its materials to make a note-book primer of your own.

Before enrolling in a language class, inquire discreetly as to the qualifications of the teacher—particularly his qualifications in the phonetics of the language he teaches, for without the basis of a good pronunciation no real work can be done. Beware of the teacher who sticks to the book. Question the wisdom of learning paradigms for homework. Insist that language is for *use*, and that the using of the one you are learning shall not be too long delayed. If you find you are learning nothing, blame neither the language nor your own incapacity. Re-consider your motive. Do you really want to learn this language ? If you genuinely do, go home and start teaching yourself.

Ultimately, that is what all adults have to do. Adult language-study is mostly self-study. In some of the ensuing chapters I propose to give advice as to the learning of particular languages ; here I shall content myself with a few general pointers.

We will assume that you are going to visit the country where the language is spoken. You will therefore require far more than a reading knowledge. A writing knowledge will hardly matter at all. But it is essential that you speak a little and understand a lot. Learning to speak and learning to understand are two separate techniques. Men excel at the first and women at the second, women having intuition on their side. Many learners become discouraged because, having attained a fair fluency in speech, they understand far less than they think they ought when they listen to the radio or a café altercation. They should not be discouraged. Anybody can speak if he has in his own hands the control of structures and vocabulary ; he cannot control what the native speaker says. Some languages are easier to understand than to speak : Dutch and German are two good examples ; German in particular does not slur its phonemes nor insist on great speed. On the other hand, French—because of its tendency to elision and nervous rapidity—is difficult to understand when spoken. That is why so many good English speakers of French like to keep talking all the time.

You are going to visit this foreign country in the summer. The time to start work seriously is after Christmas. First, if you have a new alphabet to learn (as with Russian), learn the alphabet before you learn anything else. Remember that it is only an alphabet. It is not the body and soul of the language, only its dress. If the Russians were to conquer Britain, the British might have to write English in the Cyrillic alphabet. And so imagine that this has happened ; write English names and words in Cyrillic. Do not trouble about learning Russian handwriting ; it will be enough if you can manage a decent print script. Start your new diary in Cyrillic script ; use it as a code. A strange alphabet is never really so strange : it is amazing how quickly it will yield its mysteries.

Your next task gets closer to the heart of the language—the skin, the flesh under the clothes of the alphabet. I refer to pronunciation, and would emphasise again and again and again that nothing is more important than to acquire a set of foreign phonemes that shall be entirely acceptable to your hosts. It is so important that it is better to know twenty words with a perfect accent than 20,000 with the sorry apology that contents most English people. The English have produced the finest playwrights and the finest actors in the world, yet they still see it as somehow unnatural, even effeminate, to speak anything without the accent that their mothers or their public schools bestowed on them. Yet, if an Englishman is telling a funny story that is designed to disparage a foreign race, he will find little difficulty in contriving a comic, but quire passable, pastiche of the foreign accent involved. Speaking a foreign language is a kind of acting, a kind of imitation of a foreign person. It is not, however, funny when everybody else speaks in that way ; it is we who become funny in persisting with our own native phonemes.

I might say here that a curious phenomenon in language classes run in Britain is the tendency of students to spoil their phonetic advantages by considering that a language class is a sort of social occasion. I refer, of course, to those dialect speakers who are equipped already with fine continental vowel-sounds (think of the Northern /a/, /o/, /e:/, /ɛ:/— perfect for French). These people decide to put on a ' posh ', ' hot-potato ' accent when in the company of the strangers who are the other students of the class, and this, inevitably, is used when they are asked to speak the foreign language they are there to learn. It was a Lancashireman who noted, after a visit to France, that foreigners ' speak broad '. We must speak broad with them.

To master foreign pronunciation is not so difficult. First, we must listen—to broadcasts, to gramophone records, to the foreigners them-selves, if there are any in exile among us. We will note that every language has its own phonetic trade-mark : English is full of the sound /ə/ ; French is heavily nasalised ; German has a sobbing intonation ; Russian is mad about palatalising everything ; Malay will not explode its plosives. Let us learn these tricks and apply them to English. More, let us use foreign phonemes and none else when we are speaking English. Let us pretend we are Frenchmen or Russians or Germans or Malays speaking English. This will give us fluency and relieve us from the need of thinking about too many things at the same time. It is murderous to try to juggle with a foreign vocabulary, foreign structures, foreign phonemes, foreign intonations—all at the same time—but not difficult to speak English with a foreign accent. It is an act, it is comic, but it is a very valuable exercise.

Let us make sure first that we understand exactly what these foreign phonemes are. With the minimal phonetic information that is given in the first part of this book, any student should be able to find his way about the human mouth. If his foreign language primer tells him that ' the letter " i " in Middle Low Slobovian is like the sound in English sea , " we ", " three ", but shorter and tenser ', he will know that he is facing an /i/ that is pretty close to Cardinal Vowel Number 1. If his

Russian primer tells him that ' the symbol ь softens the sound after which it appears ', he should cry out for more information, write to the publisher, ring up the author, demand a scientific description. If his French book says that *thé* is pronounced very much like English ' Tay ', he should ask for his money back. One has a right to an accurate description of the phonemic system of the language one is learning, and accuracy does not necessarily mean the use of scientific terms. To describe the ' ll ' of English ' belly ' as a singing sound and the ' ll ' of Welsh ' Llanelly ' as a blowing sound is good enough. To describe one of the Arabic back consonants as a ' dry gargle ' is excellent.

When one is familiar with the sounds of the foreign language and, as far as possible, the intonations (much listening is needed here), a start can be made on the language itself. Let us not be told what words we need to learn first ; we ought to know. Remember, though, that we are not machines trying to make a factual communication with other machines: we are concerned with establishing contact with human beings, convincing them that we too (who are now foreigners) are also human beings. Polite, smiling, friendly, deferential (where deference is called for), we are also courting sympathy and help. We need the following utterances before we need any other :

Excuse me, sir, madam, comrade, comrades, ladies, gentlemen.
I'm a (British, Irish, English, Scottish, Welsh) tourist.
I don't speak your language very well.

With these we can practise pronunciation. We need to get them right. We shall have to use them often.

In expressing our particular need, we must learn a sentence-frame—
I'm looking for . . .
Where is . . . (?)
Where, please, can I find . . . (?)

—and, to fit into that frame, various words and expressions :

a taxi ; a doctor ; a chemist ; a tobacconist ; a café ; a porter
the Hotel Splendide ; the Bureau de Change ; the ladies' toilet

After this we must learn ' Thank you very much '.

Other frames follow :

I would like . . .
My wife would like . . .
We would like . . .

And these are completed with terms like

some tea ; some coffee ; some beer ; some wine ; some caviare ; an omelette ; a bottle of brandy

Other words begin to suggest themselves now—demonstratives like ' this ', ' that ' ; the copula (' is ', ' are '), if it exists in the language you are studying ; adjectives like ' hot ', ' cold ', ' red ', ' white ' ; the numerals up to ten. Now, too, we are in a position to complete our phatic battery with ' Good morning ', ' good evening ', ' how are you ? ' and so on.

We have made a beginning. Our few simple frames can be completed with a host of nouns and phrases, and it is time now to say something about the learning of vocabulary. First, let us not subscribe to the notion that, although we cannot always think of the right word in our own language, we must nevertheless never fumble in a foreign one. We use ' er ', ' what's-it ', ' thingummy ' to fill in our gaps ; one of our first tasks must be to find out the equivalents for those in the language we are learning. Fumbling for a word is everybody's linguistic birth-right.

Next, we have to devise techniques for learning vocabulary. In succeeding chapters I shall try to show how the English-speaking peoples are helped in learning the vocabulary of both Romance and Germanic languages by their own twin heritage—English being a Germanic language with a large Latin vocabulary. But what do we do when the language we are learning is utterly and completely foreign, totally outside the linguistic family to which English belongs ? It is now that we have to use our most cunning and ingenious techniques. Let me draw on my own experience when, in early middle age, I had to learn Malay very quickly.

I have no very special linguistic aptitude ; moreover, I have a very bad memory. And so I resort to the most fantastic of mnemonics. The word for ' if ' in Malay is *kalau*. This is easy enough. Kipling wrote ' If ' ; ' Kipling ' rhymes with ' stripling ' ; a stripling is a callow person; ' callow ' is close to *kalau*. The two other, more literary, words for ' if ' are *jikalau* and *jika*, easily remembered when one has planted the strong mnemonic root of the basic word. Some mnemonics are essentially personal. *Kawan* is ' friend ' : I had a friend called Cowan. Others are ultra-ingenious. *Bermastautin* is borrowed from Arabic and means ' to settle in a country, be domiciled '. I formed an image of a stout-drinking Scotsman lying in somebody's else's bed, saying ' Ah'm settled here. Bear ma stout in '. To remember *mualíf*, another Arabic loan-word meaning an editor of a newspaper, I had to make a tortuous rhyme :

' If you've been drinking, chew a leaf
Of mint before visiting the *mualif*.'

This had to be pinned down in my head with an image of a hard-drinking newspaper reporter. I pride myself upon being able to devise mnemonics (some of them so childish as to be shameful) for any foreign word in existence.

Russian is a language that, though it belongs to the Indo-European family, contains many hard words, hard to learn and to remember. We can dispose of words like *brat*, meaning ' brother ' (' my brat of a brother '), and *sad*, meaning *garden* (' a flowerless garden is a sad sight ') with little enough trouble, but have to think hard with words like the following :

nozh—knife (try ' Eat your nosh with a knife ')
vodá—water (try ' Mr K. is so fiery, he turns water to vodka ')
karandásh—pencil (try ' Get into the car and dash off that note with a pencil ')
sobaka—dog (try ' That dog is *so* much of a *barker* ' or ' That dog is a sob-barker ' or ' So bark a number of dogs ')

Such a technique will not suit everybody, but I am persuaded that all language-learners need a mnemonic system of some kind.

The learning of autosemantic words—nouns, verbs, adjectives—is, of course, a great deal easier than learning such helper-words as ' with '. ' like ', ' when ', ' in ', especially as there is rarely any total correspondence between English and foreign usage (e.g. French *dans* cannot invariably translate English ' in '). Moreover, such words seem to lack body, to be too frail and elusive to be memorable. Russian helper-words, for instance, often consist of single phonemes—*i* (' and ') ; *v* (' in ') ; *s* (' with ', ' from ', ' since '). I suggest the composition of mnemonic rhymes. For any foreign student of English, the following should help to fix the spatial prepositions :

Out of the station puffs the train,
Under the bridge, then *up* the hill,

Down the hill, *across* the plain,
Through a village, *past* a mill,
Beside a river, till once again
It comes *to* a station and stands still.

Meanwhile, read. The *Bantam* dual language books and the *Penguin* anthologies of foreign verse are cheap and useful. They have literal translations next to the text. Whatever the view of poetry held by the average Englishman, most other peoples are fond of it. Read a French poem in a French café, and people will applaud. Read a Russian poem to Russians, and they will kiss you and buy you drinks. Learn short poems by heart. That is a sure way into the heart of the language and the hearts of the people.

TWO

LANGUAGE FAMILIES

YOU have met, in these pages, occasional references to the Aryan or Indo-Germanic or Indo-European ' family of languages '. The time has come to say briefly what this means and how it concerns us as language-learners.

We have to imagine, in that prehistoric past which is really a pre-alphabetic past, a race—shadowy, dim, unknown, but undoubtedly real—which spread all over Europe and even further East, taking its language with it—a language which, because of the normal processes of linguistic change and the fact of geographical isolation, gradually split itself up into the main languages of Europe and India. Scholars of Hitler's Germany tried to persuade the world to call this race the ' Aryan ' race (*Arya* is the Sanskrit for ' noble ' or ' excellent ') and even told the world what this race looked like—fair, tall, muscular—and what its qualities were—athletic, powerful, warlike. The image of the ' Aryans ' was very much the official Nazi image of the Germans them-selves. Because of the suspect nature of all Nazi scholarship, which was racialism in disguise, nobody has cared much to use the term ' Aryan ' any more ; even the term ' Indo-Germanic ' implied that, because German scholars had done so much work in establishing the existence of a common ancestor for several European languages, the German nation had the right to plant its flag in the name to be given to this language. ' Indo-European ' is accurate enough (though it leaves Persian out of the picture) and it is the term we shall use here.

Though the Indo-European language no longer exists (it split up before writing was invented), we cannot doubt the thesis that it was there, very solidly, in pre-history, the mother of the major languages of the modern West *in potentia*, disclosing itself shadowily to-day through the kinship that exists—sometimes under a mask—in those very languages. Just as English ' milk ' is like German *Milch*, ' bread ' like *Brot*, and ' water ' like *Wasser*, so ' father ' is like German *Vater*, Dutch *vader*, Gothic *fadar*, Old Norse *faðir*, Greek and Latin *pater*,

Sanskrit *pitar*; and 'brother' resembles Dutch *broeder*, German *Bruder*, Greek *phrater*, Latin *frater*, Sanskrit *bhratar*, Russian *brat*, Irish *brathair*. In other words, there is a family face, and from it one may even learn how to recontruct probable forms in the ancient mother-language. Thus, the Indo-European for 'father' must have begun with a lip-sound ; the middle consonant must have been dental or alveolar ; there must have been a final r-sound. Again, the ancient form for 'brother' must have had an initial lip-sound, then an r-sound, a back vowel, a dental or alveolar consonant, a front vowel and a final 'r'.

That, of course, would be the mere root of the word, for we cannot doubt that this ancient language was, like Latin and Greek, rich in inflexions, with special forms for 'to a brother', 'from a brother', 'with brothers', 'of brothers', and so on. In the late eighteenth century European scholars began to look at Sankrit—that ancient language of India—and, in the nineteenth century, a dim notion of what Indo-European must have been like in its conjugations and declensions was formed from the rich grammar of the Indic tongue. Sankrit has a far older literature than either Latin or Greek, and thus, in it, we can see what must be features of the mother-language more fully preserved than in either of the two classical European tongues. Here is the verb 'to be' (present tense) in Sanskrit and some of its sister languages :

Anglo-Saxon	Gothic	Latin	Greek	Sanskrit
eom (am)	im	sum	eimi	asmi
eart (art)	is	es	ci	asi
is (is)	ist	est	csti	asti
sindon (are)	sijum	sumus	esmen	smas
sindon (are)	sijuth	estis	este	stha
sindon (are)	sind	sunt	eisi	santi

We shrug our shoulders at the irregularities we find in our verbs to-day ; it is interesting to note that, the further back we go, the more irregularities tend to disappear : the present tense of the verb 'to be' in Sanskrit is no different in its endings from other Sanskrit verbs. Here is the present tense of 'to give', with the Greek beside it for comparison :

Sanskrit		Greek
dadami	(I give)	didomi
dadasi	(thou givest)	didos

Sanskrit		*Greek*
dadati	(he gives)	didosi
dadmas	(we give)	didomen (*dialect* didomes)
dattha	(you give)	didote
dadati	(they give)	didoasi (*dialect* didonti)

When the study of the Indo-European family of languages got under way—early in the nineteenth century—a natural division was made between the ' older ' languages—Latin, Greek, and Sanskrit—and the ' younger ' Germanic ones. It was recognised—for, after all, this was a process that went on in recorded history—that Spanish, Italian, Portuguese, French were derived from Latin ; it was similarly recognised that German, Dutch, English, Gothic, and the Scandinavian languages had a common origin in a primitive Germanic tongue which was lost (like the Indo-European language itself) because of lack of written records. But this primitive Germanic language could be guessed at as to its shape and content, and it seemed to be a ' young ' language, one that had broken away from the older forms represented by Latin, Greek, and Sanskrit.

Jacob Grimm—one of the Brothers Grimm who produced the very grim fairy tales—formulated, in 1822, a law which accounted for the consonantal differences between Germanic and the older tongues. Really, he was trying to answer the question ' Why, if the Germanic and the classical tongues have a common origin, is "brother" (or *Bruder*) so different from *frater*, " father " (or *Vater*) so different from *pater* and so on ? Why these big consonantal differences at the beginning and in the middle of words which are supposed to be fundamentally the same ? ' Grimm's Law could not explain, but it could formulate ; it could show that the Germanic language, in separating itself from the ' classical' phase of Indo-European, had followed at least a regular pattern of consonantal change. The pattern can be summed up as follows :

The area of articulation of a consonant in the ' classical ' phase of Indo-European does not change when Germanic comes into being : a labial sound in Latin, Greek, or Sanskrit corresponds to a labial sound in Germanic ; a dental or alveolar consonant remains dental or alveolar ; a velar consonant remains velar. If the following list represents the main consonants in these groups, then the changes will be horizontal, not vertical :

	Unvoiced	Voiced	Fricative
Labial	p	b	f (v)
Dental	t	d	th (z)
Velar	k (c)	g	ch (/x/) or h

Let us see how this works out in practice :

Classical	Germanic
Greek, Latin *pater*	father
Latin *pulex*	flea
Latin *frango*	break
Greek *odont-*, Latin *dent-*	tooth, *Zahn*
Latin *tenuis*	thin
Greek *kard-*, Latin *cord-*	heart, *Harz*
Latin *octo*	eight, *acht*
Latin *hortus*	garden, *Garten*
Greek *gonu*, Latin *genu*	knee
Greek *thugater*	daughter
Latin *fero*	bear

The rule seems to apply well enough : one kind of labial in the classical languages will correspond to a different kind of labial in the Germanic languages (here represented only by English and German), and the same will apply to the other areas of articulation.

Grimm's Law did not seem to give a totally satisfactory answer to many inquirers. For instance, why should the ' t ' in *pater* correspond to the ' th ' in ' father ', but the ' t ' in Latin *centum* correspond to the ' d ' in ' hundred ' ? Surely, if the law is to apply consistently, the English word should be ' hunthred ' ? The Dutchman Karl Verner proposed, in 1875, a law of his own to explain seeming irregularities like that. It was all a matter of accentuation, he said. Indo-European ' k ', ' t ', ' p ' became ' h ', ' th ', ' f ' respectively in Germanic if the original accent was on the preceding syllable. But, if the accent was originally on a different syllable, the sounds became voiced—' g ', ' d ', ' b '. Granted that *centum* is pronounced with the accent on the second syllable, the correspondence of ' t ' with English ' d ' in ' hundred ' is quite regular.

There is, of course, much more to these laws—Grimm's and Verner's—than can be presented here. Indeed, the modern student of language may be prepared to question the validity of linguistic laws that were formulated before Phonetics existed as a science. But it is important to think in terms of regular laws of change when studying languages : the seeming caprice, the baffling irregularity, can always be explained. More, a knowledge of laws of sound-change helps us to ease our language-learning task, as we shall see later.

Let us now briefly see what languages make up the great Indo-European group. The long-dead mother left behind nine tongues which have, in their turn, split up into a number of languages spoken to-day. The nine principal groups corresponding to the nine old daughter-languages are : Indian, Iranian, Armenian, Hellenic, Albanian, Italic, Balto-Slavic, Germanic, and Celtic.

The great Indian language, Sanskrit, is, as we have already noted, the oldest surviving language of the Indo-European group. Its sacred writings go back as far as 1500 B.C., and it is still read, chiefly by devout Hindus and students of Hinduism. An important Western poem, T. S. Eliot's *The Waste Land,* bases its final section on three injunctions from the *Upanishads—Datta* (' give '), *Dayadhvam* (' sympathise '), *Damyata* (' control ')—and ends with a triple Sanskrit blessing : *Shantih. Shantih. Shantih.* Sanskrit, like Latin, ceased to be a spoken language while it was still flourishing as a language of ritual and prayer. The local dialects that used to flourish alongside of Sanskrit have survived to become the living tongues of some hundreds of millions of Indians (one of them—Pali—has become also a literary and sacred language, the official tongue of the Buddhists). The main ones are Hindi, Bengali, Punjabi, and Mahrati. The Hindustani that, to most Englishmen, is the lingua franca of the country (especially the North), is a mixture of Hindi, Persian, and Arabic. Words like ' chit ', ' pukka ', ' chota peg ', ' wallah ', and so on are now established as part of the heritage of English, and they come from Hindustani. The tongue of the Gypsies—Romany—is a dialect of north-western India which, with the wanderers who speak it, has spread not only through Europe but into America as well. It is no mere ' thieves' slang ' : it is a genuine and ancient member of the Indian group of languages.

Iranian splits into two parts—the eastern language known as Avestan (or Zend, though this is not strictly accurate) which takes its name from the *Avesta*—the sacred book of the Zoroastrians ; the western language known as Old Persian, which is preserved only in the records of the achievements of Darius and Xerxes, some 500 years before Christ. Out of Old Persian developed Pahlavi, which is the ancestor of the Persian spoken to-day. There is a good deal of Arabic in Persian, and the alphabet itself is Arabic, but there is no doubt of the Indo-European roots of what must be the simplest language of all for the Westerner to learn. The following words disguise very recognisable forms (read from right to left) :

دختر   برادر

r t kh d   r d a r b

مادر

r d a m

—' brother ', ' daughter ', and ' mother ', in fact.

Armenian is spoken round the Black Sea and the Caucasus, and it probably got there about seven centuries before Christ. It seems to have crossed the Hellespont to get there, and there is evidence that the ancient languages Phrygian (the speakers of which were the Homeric Trojans) and Macedonian resemble it somewhat. Modern Armenian, which has a large but not world-shattering literature, has been much influenced by Persian and it has also come into contact with certain Semitic languages, as well as Greek and Turkish. But under the very mixed vocabulary the Indo-European origin shines clear. (Armenian, like English and Persian, has dropped grammatical gender.)

The Hellenic group is large and complex. The Hellenes—or Greeks—entered the Aegean area about 2000 B.C. and spread into the mainland of Greece, as well as on to the Aegean islands and the coast of Asia Minor. The older languages—Lydian, Lycian, Carian, Hittite—went under, and the four Hellenic dialect groups—Ionic (of which Attic was a member), Aeolic, Arcadian-Cyprian, and Doric—took control. Attic, being the dialect of the city-state of Athens, became the most important for obvious reasons—the commercial and political power of Athens, the great dramatists, philosophers, orators, and historians who wrote in Attic. The Attic dialect became the *koiné* or popular Greek which survives in the New Testament and in the Byzantine literature of Constantinople. It split up, over the course of the centuries, into the demotic Greek spoken by the ordinary people of Greece to-day, and the so-called 'pure' Greek of the schools, newspapers, and serious poets and novelists.

Albanian is spoken on the east coast of the Adriatic—the language of that Illyria which is the locale of Shakespeare's *Twelfth Night*. It has no great literature and its vocabulary is so bastard a mixture of Latin, Greek, Turkish, and Slavonic that it is rather difficult to dig out the original elements. Nevertheless, it is an original member of the Indo-European family.

The Italic group began, as the name indicates, in Italy. We must guard against identifying the Latin, or Romance, group with it, for Latin was once merely one of the old Italic dialects : it later became important because, as with Attic Greek, important or at least energetic people spoke it. Other Italic tongues were Umbrian and Oscan, and there was a language—now almost completely lost but certainly not Indo-European—called Etruscan used by a vigorous people that left something of its art behind. The district of Latium contained Rome, and its language became increasingly inportant as Rome's political influence grew. Latin became the tongue of an Empire, and it is still, in one form or another, with us at the present day. The daughters of Latin require, in fact, a whole chapter to themselves, and they will get it later.

The Baltic and Slavic languages are sufficiently like each other to justify our putting them into a common group. The Baltic languages are, however, of much more philological than literary, social, or political interest. German ousted what was once a lively Baltic language—Prussian—in the seventeenth century ; Lettic is spoken by a couple of million people in Latvia. Lithuanian is of immense value to the language scholar because, of all living Indo-European tongues, it seems to conserve most of the elements of the ancient mother-tongue. It is said that a Sanskrit scholar can make himself understood in a Lithuanian village.

The Slavic group contains the giant Russian. This was first written down by St Cyril (who gave it the Cyrillic script) in the ninth century, in the form of Old Church Slavonic or Old Bulgarian—a South Slavic which is not too different from the old East Slavic which is the official mother of Great Russian. Great Russian (or just ' Russian ') is obviously of immense and growing importance. Little Russian, or Ukrainian, is considered by the Ukrainians themselves to be an important branch of the Slavic original, and they emphasise its distinctness from the official tongue of the Kremlin, but with little justice. White Russian is found in Western Russia and adjacent parts of Poland, and it is the mother-tongue of some 5,000,000 people.

Polish is the most important language of the West Slavic sub-group, followed by Czecho-Slovakian. Sorbian or Wend is to be found in Germany, near Dresden, but it serves as the mother-tongue of less than 1,000,000. In South Slavic we have Bulgarian, Serbo-Croatian, and Slovenian—these last two spoken within the new holiday-maker's region of Jugoslavia. All these Slavic tongues are very much like each other—far more like each other than English is like German, for instance—and to learn one is to half-learn the others. The pan-Slav concept is very real as far as the languages of the Slavs are concerned.

The Teutonic or Germanic group of languages will require a chapter to itself. Its importance need not be emphasised here, as it contains both English and German, but we ought to note how the whole Teutonic family is divided. East Teutonic contained Gothic, the language of a powerful and aggressive people which survives in some fragments of Biblical translation carried out in the fourth century by Bishop Ulfilas (a Greek). In the same group were Burgundian and Vandalic, but these have not survived at all. There is a moral here somewhere. Despite the depredations of the Goths and the Vandals, the Latin language flourished. Conquerors seem to need a literature if they are to eternise their language. North Teutonic contains the tongues of Scandinavia— Swedish and Danish to the east, Norwegian and Icelandic to the west. We still think it important to learn Old Icelandic for the sake of the sagas. West Teutonic covers two branches—High and Low German, which came into being as separate sub-groups about 600 A.D., when a sound-shift rather like that ancient one described by Grimm started to operate. The old Low German tongues were Old Saxon, Old Low Franconian, Old Frisian, and Old English (or Anglo-Saxon). Out of Old Saxon came the modern *Plattdeutsch*, the homely day-to-day language of many Germans ; Old Low Franconian turned into modern Dutch and Flemish ; Frisian survives in Friesland and a few small islands. High German—which is divided into Old High German, Middle

High German, and Modern High German—has become the official and literary language of Germany : it is what we mean when we talk of ' German '. It first gained its hold in the sixteenth century, when Luther translated his Bible into it.

The last of the Indo-European groups is the Celtic one, whose decline and fall makes a curious and sad story. Two thousand years ago the Celts were everywhere—France, Spain, Britain, Germany, Northern Italy ; they had even, in the centuries before Christ, advanced into Greece and Asia Minor. But recorded history shows the Celtic languages giving way all over—Gallic in France replaced by Latin, Cymric (or Britannic Celtic) driven west by the Teuton invader, Welsh and Erse and Gaelic losing ground to English, Cornish dying out completely. Nationalistic movements in the ' Celtic fringe ' of England have succeeded in reviving dying tongues, but it would be idle to pretend that such shots-in-the-arm can do more than provide energy for waving a feeble banner.

These, then, are the languages of the Indo-European family. This, it will be noticed, by no means accounts for all the living tongues of Europe. Lappish, Finnish, Esthonian, Magyar (Hungarian) form a family of their own, called Finno-Ugrian. The language of Malta falls into that Semitic group which also contains Arabic, Ethiopian, Hebrew. The old ' sick man of Europe ', Turkey, takes its language from that Turco-Tartar family which gives Tartar and Kirghiz. But, you will note, the motif of family, of relationship, prevails. Go East, and Chinese will be seen to be part of the Indo-Chinese family, along with Tibetan, Siamese, and Burmese. Malay in all its forms belongs with Fijian, Tahitian and Maori—the Malayo-Polynesian group. To know what family a language belongs to is a huge help in learning it. To an Englishman, Frenchman, Greek, the task of learning Russian will be eased once the fact of its Indo-European nature is known. There will be genders, declensions, conjugations, and these conjugations will have a flavour of Latin or Sanskrit about them. Tackle Finnish and we are up against new territory, new principles—agglutination, word-building. The Semitic languages will behave mysteriously, staking out their three consonants to make a kind of word-ghost. Chinese will behave most mysteriously of all, clinging to single syllables and tones.

Let us look now at a few of the more important languages of the Indo-European family, starting with the ones that are closest to English.

THREE

THE TONGUE OF THE BRITISH

THE English call themselves British, but the true British are the Welsh. Those Ancient Britons whom the Romans fought and subdued— Boadicea is a Welsh heroine, not an English one—were driven to Wales (' land of the foreigner ') by the invading Anglo-Saxons. English is a foreign language as far as Britain is concerned. Welsh, or Cymric, was the tongue for many centuries of what is now called England. King Arthur held back the barbarous invader for as long as he could, in the name of the Christian Roman Empire. He was a Romanised Welshman ; the barbarous invaders spoke the ancestor of the language I am writing now. These facts ought to be pondered on occasionally. The Welsh language, dying, kept artificially alive in schools and eisteddfodau, deserves our respect and our homage.

The big difficulty that presents itself to the learner of Welsh is the tendency of nouns to change their initial sounds in the phenomenon known as *mutation*. This means that a dictionary is quite useless until we are well into the language : we cannot, as we can with almost any other Indo-European tongue, start reading right away. Look up *gadair* (' chair ') or *bib* (' pipe ') in a Welsh–English dictionary and you will find no entry. These, in fact, are mutations of the forms *cadair* and *pib* respectively.

Welsh has no indefinite article (' a ' or ' an ') but it has a definite article—*y, yr,* or *'r*. This causes mutations of the so-called ' soft ' variety :

tref—a town	*y dref*—the town
basged—a basket	*y fasged*—the basket
desg—a desk	*y ddesg*—the desk
gardd—a garden	*yr ardd*—the garden

In the same way, soft mutation takes place with adjectives when these qualify a feminine noun :

llyfr bach—a little book	*fferm fach*— a little farm

hogyn drwg—a naughty boy   *geneth ddrwg*—a naughty girl
dwr poeth—hot water   *teisen boeth*—a hot cake

In addition, there are nasal mutation and spirant mutation, so that many words appear under four distinct forms (including the radical, or dictionary form). Look up ' horse ' in the English–Welsh section of a dictionary and you will find *ceffyl*. But 'his horse' is *ei geffyl* (soft mutation), ' my horse ' is *fy ngheffyl* (nasal mutation), and ' her horse ' is *ei cheffyl* (spirant mutation). Similarly, the radical *tad* means ' father ', but we talk of ' his *dad* ', ' her *thad* ', and ' my *nhad* '.

Not even the numerals are free from this initial consonantal change. *Un cant* is ' one hundred ' (there is a shining indication of the Indo-Germanic origins of Welsh), but note the following :

> 200—*dau gant*
> 300—*tri chant* (*ch*, as in German, = /x/)
> 400—*pedwar cant*
> 500—*pum cant*
> 600—*chwe chant*

The *g*, *c* (/k/), and *ch* (/x/) are, of course, all velar forms, so that the mutation (look back at Grimm's Law) is ' horizontal '. But the change from *mil* (1,000) to *dwy fil* (2,000) can only be explained in terms of a bilabial fricative (/β/) bridging the gap between *m* and *f* (/v/).

This sensitivity of initial consonants in Welsh may be regarded as the trade-mark of its syntax, just as the unvoiced L (*ll* = /ḷ/) is the most idiosyncratic feature of its phonology. But to learners of Welsh there are attractive simplicities hardly to be found in other Indo-European languages. It is possible, for instance, to make any present tense form with the verb *bod* (' to be ') and a present participle made out of an infinitive (' *darllen*—' to read ' ; *yn darllen*—' reading '). The present tense of *bod* is as follows :

> *yr wyf i*—I am
> *yr wyf ti*—thou art   *yr ydym ni*—we are
> *y mae ef*—he is   *yr ydych chwi*—you are
> *y mae hi*—she is   *y maent hwy*—they are

The article *y* or *yr* has no meaning here, incidentally. Note that the pronoun comes after the verb. This is characteristic of Welsh, which prefers the following word-order : (1) Verb ; (2) Subject ; (3) Object ;

(4) the rest of the sentence. ' I am reading ' or ' I read ' is rendered as
Yr wyf i'n (i yn) darllen. ' We are learning to read ' is *Yr ydym ni'n
(ni yn) dysgu darllen.* A special form of the third person singular of
bod—indifferently singular and plural—is used when a noun governs
it as subject :

> *Y mae'r bachgen yn gweithio*—the boy is working
> *Y mae'r bechgyn yn chwarae*—the boys are playing

The vocabulary of Welsh is naturally rich, but it absorbed, under the
Roman occupation, a fair number of Latin words :

llyfr—book (*liber*)	*pobl*—people (*populus*)
eglwys—church (*ecclesia*)	*pont*—bridge (*pont-*)
mur—wall (*murus*)	*gwin*—wine (*vinum*)
ffenestr—window (*fenestra*)	*coron*—crown (*corona*)

Inevitably, too, there are plenty of English loan-words :

bag	*desg* (desk)
banc (bank)	*ffatri* (factory)
basn (basin)	*ffilm* (film)
beisicl (bicycle)	*inc*
brecwast (breakfast)	*lamp*
busnes (business)	*map*
bws (bus)	*papur*
cwnstabl (constable)	*plismon* (policeman)

But the Welsh language has left its mark on a number of placenames
in England, as, indeed, the various forms of old Celtic have survived in
quite unexpected parts of Europe. ' Water ' is /dur/—*dwr* in Welsh—
and it can be seen clearly enough in the following : Dour, Douro,
Derwent, Dorchester, Dordogne. An alternative word for ' water '
appears in the non-Cymric forms of Celtic as *uisge* ; Welsh has *wysg*.
The root is to be seen in the following : Esk, Usk, Isis, Exe, Ouse,
Ischia, Aisne, Ausonne, Oise. The Welsh for ' river ' is *afon* (/avon/),
and cognate Celtic forms are found in these names : Aisne, Ain,
Vienne. ' Avon,' then, is not so much the name of particular rivers as
the term for ' river ' in general.

Here, now, are some Welsh words which, on the surface, do not seem to resemble any of the corresponding words in the Indo-European languages which are best known :

anadl—breath	*eira*—snow
annwyd—cold	*gair*—word
arian—money	*haul*—sun
brenin—king	*ia*—ice
blodeuyn—flower	*llaeth*—milk
bwyd—food	*llong*—ship
coeden—tree	*plentyn*—child
chwaer—sister	*telyn*—harp
diolch—thanks	*wythnos*—week

Out of *haul* and *llaeth* emerge the ghosts of *helios* (as in ' heliograph ') and *lact-* (as in ' lactic '), but we are given no help from other languages in trying to master the other words. There is a hard lesson to be learned here. We have seen, in the section on Semantic Change, how the Italian *cattivo* (' bad ') comes from Latin *captivus* (' captive '). The simple-minded might expect the Italian to develop the Latin *malus* (as the French language has done with *mal*). But, almost accidentally, a language will build its vocabulary out of what takes its fancy, choosing among a wide range of synonyms or even perverting, limiting, or extending the meaning of a word which lies quite outside the semantic area involved. It is not so much vocabulary that indicates origin as structure, and the structure of Welsh is thoroughly Indo-European.

Welsh is no longer a major language, but it has produced—and is still producing—a considerable literature. Unfortunately, the major literary talents of Wales turn to English, and we can be fairly sure that no modern Welsh-writing poet can match the achievement of, say, Dylan Thomas, who knew little Welsh but brought a Welsh ' bardic ' quality to English verse. Still, there is an untranslatable charm in Welsh lyrical poetry, and the following folk song stanza will serve as a fair specimen :

> *Ffarwel i blwyf Llangower,*
> *A'r Bala dirion deg ;*
> *Ffarwel fy annwyl gariad,*
> *Nid wyf yn enwi neb.*

It is worthwhile to learn this by heart. The pronunciation of the vowels follows the Continental or Latin pattern. *W* is a vowel symbol, standing for /u/ ; *y* after *w* is /i/, otherwise it approaches /ə/. *Ll*, of course, stands for the unvoiced L—/ḷ/—while /v/ is shown as *f* and /f/ as *ff*. The Welsh lilt, so different from the English tendency to monotone, may be picked up from the radio or television. Now for the words and their meanings.

Ffarwel (trilled ' r ' and clear ' l ') is a loan-word—' farewell '.

i is a preposition—' to '.

blwyf is a mutated form of *plwyf*—' parish ' ; the soft mutation has been brought about by the preceding *i*.

Llangower is a place-name.

a'r is a combination of *a* (' and ') and *yr* (' the ').

Bala is a place-name.

dirion is a soft mutation of *tirion* (' gentle ').

deg is a soft mutation of *teg* (' lovely '). Both adjectives qualify *Bala*.

fy is ' my '.

annwyl is ' dear '.

gariad is a soft mutation of *cariad* (' sweetheart '). The mutation is the responsibility of the preceding adjective.

nid is ' not '.

wyf is the middle portion of *yr wyf i*—' I am '.

yn enwi is a combination of the untranslatable present participle signaller *yn* and the infinitive *enwi* (' to name '). This gives ' naming ', ' giving the name of '.

neb is ' nobody '.

The whole quatrain therefore reads : ' Farewell to the parish of Llangower and to gentle, lovely Bala. Farewell to my dear sweetheart (I'm not naming anybody).'

The remaining stanza tells of going, with 'heart like lead', to live in the ' land of the Saxon '. Here, for English people, is the other side of the moon.

FOUR

LEARNING TEUTONIC LANGUAGES

FROM even the flimsy survey of the Welsh language we have just made, it will be clear that Welsh is close to English only in a geographical sense. In comparison with Welsh, which came to England in prehistoric times, English is very much an ' imported ' language, and it has to leap back into Europe to find its near relatives. Though the Norman Conquest, and subsequent scholastic devotion to Latin, have given English the surface appearance of a Romance language, it is very much a Germanic dialect.

What is a dialect, and what is a language ? My wife was born in South Wales ; I was born in Manchester. We went to live for a time in a small village near Preston, Lancashire. When we entered a pub one rainy day, my wife was greeted by the landlord with the words ' Art witshert ? ' (/aˑt 'wɪtʃət ?/) I understood this, but my wife did not. It is a way of saying ' Are your feet wet ? ' (' Art thou wet-shod ? ') Later the landlord said of his own wife : ' Oo's getten showder-wartsh ' (/ʊːz 'gɛtn 'ʃaʊdə waˑtʃ/), meaning ' She's got a pain in her shoulder '. Again, I understood, but my wife did not. To her it was a foreign language ; to me it was a kind of English I had often heard as a child but had never consciously got down to learning. We were hearing Lancashire dialect, or rather that particular kind of Lancashire dialect spoken in the Ribble valley. Native English, then ; a tongue not spoken by foreigners. And yet, to my wife, as foreign a language as Finnish or Lithuanian.

We like to clear an English dialect of the charge of being a foreign language by pointing to elements in it that only seem foreign because they are archaic. Thus, the ' art ' of ' art tha ' in dialectal speech is a survival from what was good Queen's English in Shakespeare's time. In ' Oo's getten showder-wartsh ' we can pick out the Anglo-Saxon ' heo ' that was eventually replaced by ' she '. ' Getten ' is a form of the past participle cognate with American and Elizabethan ' gotten ' (it survives in modern Queen's English in ' forgotten ' and ' begotten ').

' Showder ' shows a development of Middle English ' schulder ' which, when one sees how ' hūs ' became ' house ' and the dark L of ' talk ' and ' alms ' disappeared, has as good a claim to be regarded as English as the standard form ' shoulder ' (/'ʃouldə/). ' Wartsh ' goes back to Anglo-Saxon ' weorc ' which, with a more generalised meaning than is found in this Lancashire form, is easily recognised as the ancestor of ' work '. All this, then, presents a paradox. Good honest native English can appear to another English-speaker as a foreign language.

The process of historical analysis is no way of separating ' foreign language ' from ' dialect '. For, if I say : *Mein Vater ist ein guter Mann* or *Der Winter ist kalt*, the meaning is clear enough to the person with no German : there are elements in both German and English which are fundamentally the same. Indeed, the two German sentences may well be more intelligible to the Southern Englishman than the two Lancashire ones I have quoted. We must conclude, perhaps, that the terms ' dialect ' and ' language ' have very indistinct boundaries, and that ' foreign ' has more social or ethnographical significance than linguistic.

The closeness of English and German is best seen in the earlier phases of the two languages. Here is some Anglo-Saxon poetry :

> Ða waes on healle   heardecg togen,
> sweord ofer setlum,   sidrand manig
> hafen handa faest :   helm no gemunde,
> byrnan side,   þa hine se broga angeat . . .
> . . . hraðe heo aeðelinga   anna haefde
> faeste befongen,   þa heo to fenne gang . . .

That is part of our national epic *Beowulf* ; it means : ' Then was in the hall the hardedged (sword) seized, the sword over the benches, many a broad shield raised firmly in the hand : helmet did not remember the wide burnie, when him the monster seized . . . quickly she of the warriors one had securely seized, when she to the fen went . . .' The ' she ' referred to is the mother of Grendel ; both are foul murderous man-eating monsters. *Beowulf*, I have always maintained, would make a first-rate horror-film. Here for comparison, is a line or two from the German *Hildebrandslied* (' Song of Hildebrand ') :

> Ik gihorta ðat seggen,
> ðat sih urhettun . aenon muotin,

Hiltibrant enti Haðubrant . untar heriun tuem,
sunu fatar ungo . . .

(A free translation : ' I have heard it said that two chosen men, Hildebrand and Hadubrand, met in single combat between two armies, the son and the father . . .') If one wishes to learn an old Germanic language, is there much to choose between these two ?

When we look at older forms of the Germanic tongues, we tend to feel more at home than with their modern forms, chiefly because English has retained certain sounds once common to all the Germanic family but since—in all except English and Icelandic (an intensely conservative language)—shifted into sounds cognate but different. Take the two consonants /θ/ and /ð/, for instance, indifferently represented in English as ' th '. Icelandic clings to the old signs as well as the old sounds (this is from a newspaper : ' *Um 90 þusand tunnur salta ðar alls á öllu landinu og i kvöld er búist við að 200 pus . . .*') but look what has happened in German :

Dank—thanks	*Ding*—thing
dass—that	*Durst*—thirst
dann—then	*Distel*—thistle
dick—thick	*Dorn*—thorn
dünn—thin	*Dorf*—thorp = village

The initial consonant ' th ', which, in the English words above, is sometimes a symbol for /θ/, sometimes for /ð/, has an invariable equivalent of *d* in German. But in Swedish there is a differentiation, so that *t* stands for English /θ/ and *d* for English /ð/ :

tjock—thick	*det*—that
ting—thing	*dem*—them
tänka—think	*där*—there
tre—three	*fader*—father
tron—throne	*broder*—brother

Another shift that English has resisted is that from /w/ to /v/. German spelling does not show the true pronunciation of *Wasser, Wurm, Wort*, and so on (' water ', ' worm ', ' word ') ; we have to accept ' w ' as a symbol for /v/. But in Swedish the spelling is honest :

vagn—waggon	*väder*—weather
vatten—water	*väl*—well

vild—wild   *vid*—wide
verk—work   *villig*—willing
varm—warm   *ved*—wood

From this point on, we had better concentrate on German. It is, by virtue of its modern literature (from Goethe and Schiller on) as well as its philosophy and science, by far the most important language of the Germanic group (English, of course, excepted). The Scandinavian languages have their own interest, but only Ibsen and Hans Andersen are world literary figures, and they are available in translation : modern Scandinavian poetry is not, except of course, for the specialist, crying out to be read. As for Dutch, Holland shrugs its shoulders at the diminishing importance of this close relative of English ; English is spoken by all educated Lowlanders. But German cannot be ignored by anyone.

The learning of German words is eased when we remember certain sound-shifts. First, English /t/ becomes an affricate /ts/, represented in German spelling as *z* :

tap—*Zapfen*   tongue—*Zunge*   to—*zu*

This is at the beginning of words ; in the middle or at the end German goes the whole hog and has, for English /t/, a fricative—*ss* :

better—*besser*   eat—*essen*   foot—*Fuss*
kettle—*Kessel*   let—*lassen*   water—*Wasser*

(Note that German nouns begin with a capital—a time-waster to the typist.)

The English ' d ' often comes out as German ' t ' :

daughter—*Tochter*   day—*Tag*   drink—*trinken*

Two phenomena might, in addition, be noted in the above two first examples. The English ' gh ', which used to stand for /x/, is now a mere sign of vowel-length, but, in trying to sort out the meaning of a German word, it is a good plan to substitute English ' gh ' for German *ch* and see if any sense comes out of it—*Licht, lach(en), Nacht*, for example. The *g* of *Tag* has softened to ' y ' in English ' day ' ; sometimes it appears in English as ' w ' (note that both ' y ' and ' w ' are semi-vowel symbols used to indicate /ɪ/ and /ʊ/ respectively as second elements of diphthongs). Thus, if the *v* of *Vogel* is pronounced /f/, what does the whole word mean ? How about *pfennig, Bog(en), Weg* ?

The German *ch* stands for /x/ after a back vowel, /ç/ after a front one. It is sometimes equivalent to English ' k ' :

book—*Buch*	make—*machen*	week—*Woch* (/x/)
weak—*weich*	reek—*riechen*	rake—*Rechen* (/ç/)

English ' p ' either becomes the affricate *pf* (/pf/) or else the full-blown fricative ' f ' (/f/), according to position :

path—*Pfad*	pepper—*Pfeffer*	pipe—*Pfeife*
plant—*Pflanze*	sleep—*schlafen*	

This last example also reminds us that English ' s ' + consonant appears in German as /ʃ/ (spelt *sch*) + consonant :

sleep—*schlafen*	smut—*Schmutz*	snow—*Schnee*
swan—*Schwan*	sweat—*Schweiss*	

Finally, English non-initial ' v ' often appears as German *b* :

give—*geben*	have—*haben*	love—*lieben*

In addition to these disguised identities, there are several words which are patently identical in English and German, though German prefers that older pronunciation still retained in, say, Lancashire English (e.g. *Butter, Mann, hier, Lamm*). And German sometimes gives a clearer indication of the English pronunciation of a word held in common than the English spelling itself—take *Haus, Maus*, for example.

It is not really possible to work out tables of vowel equivalents for the two languages. English ' o—e ' will sometimes appear as German *ei* (/ai/), as in these examples :

one—*ein*   bone—*Bein* (leg)   home—*Heim-*

But there is no invariable rule to be made out of it. As with Semitic languages (there is a curious irony here, when one remembers the Nazi philosophy), German yields its secrets through the consonants.

One further point to be made about the German vocabulary is that it is ' pure ' : it hates to borrow from other languages. Where, for instance, English is only too ready to make its scientific words out of Greek elements (' oxygen ', ' nitrogen ', ' hydrogen '), German produces home-made terms like *Sauerstoff, Stickstoff*, and *Wasserstoff*. Even with new sciences like semantics German resists the international term and chooses *Bedeutungslehre* ('meaning-lore'), and phonetics is taught as *Lautlehre* (' sound-lore '). Much of this native Germanic vocabulary has ceased to be used in English. The ' sore ' of ' He was sore afraid ' (equivalent to German *sehr*) has been replaced by the Romance form ' very ' ; a butcher is no longer a ' flesher ' (*Fleischer*) and ' to dree ' (*drehen*) is now ' to turn '.

It is a help when reading German to think in terms of the English of Shakespeare's day (or even earlier) rather than modern English. This will help with forms like *fast* (' almost ') and *oft*. Tricks of inversion in German (' That have I oft seen ') match earlier English usage. It is good training for German speech to play the harmless trick of inversion and verb-shunting with our own language : it is not, after all, so very un-native. We are sometimes surprised to find separation of verb and defining prefix (*anzeigen*—' to advertise ' ; *Wir zeigen nicht an*—' We don't advertise '), but this is common enough in English : ' Put your hat on ' ; ' Kick the door to.' German is, when all is said and done, a dialectal kinsman of English.

The time has come to look at some German. Here is a passage from a modern poem by Friedrich Georg Jünger (born 1898). I have chosen it at random :

> *Mit dem Saft der Maulbeere haben die Kinder*
> *Ihre kleinen Gesichter beschmiert.*
> *Näscher sind sie, Koster der Süssigkeit.*
> *Sie tanzen in ihren geflickten Kleidern,*
> *Und mit ihnen tanzt der Westwind,*
> *Tanzt auf den Schnüren die Wäsche.*
> *Es ist, als ob ein Hauch des wunderbaren Lebens*
> *Die leeren Hüllen des Menschen fülle.*

After what has been said about the ultimate identity of German and English, it will be a disappointment to find words here that have no equivalent form in modern English. We have to remember again that it is all a matter of choice, of semantic change ; one language prefers to render an idea with one word, another language with another : German still uses *Tier* for ' animal ', while English took over a French word and made *Tier* (' deer ') into a particular kind of animal. Take a deep breath and look carefully here ; there are plenty of words which have maintained the same meaning, and almost the same form, in both languages. Here is a literal translation which retains the German word-order :

' With the juice of the mulberry have the children their little faces be-smeared. Fruit-stealers are they, tasters of sweetness. They dance in their patched clothing, and with them dances the west wind, dances on the lines the washing. It is as though a breath of wonderful life the empty hulls (husks) of man fills.'

And now a piece of prose, the beginning of the story *Ein Landarzt* by Franz Kafka. ' Land ' has taken on the specific meaning of ' country ' (as opposed to ' town ') in German ; a *Landarzt* is a country doctor :

Ich war in grosser Verlegenheit : eine dringende Reise stand mir bevor ; ein Schwerkranker wartete auf mich in einem zehn Meilen entfernten Dorfe ; starkes Schneegestöber füllte den weiten Raum zwischen mir und ihm ; einen Wagen hatte ich, leicht, grossräderig, ganz wie er für unsere Landstrassen taugt ; in den Pelz gepackt, die Instrumententasche in der Hand, stand ich reisefertig schon auf dem Hofe ; aber das Pferd fehlte, das Pferd . . .

Let us keep very close to the German : ' I was in gross (great) embarrassment : an urgent ride (journey) stood me before (faced me) ; a sorely-ill-one waited on (for) me in a ten mile far thorp (village) ; stark (strong, heavy) snowstorm filled the wide room (large space) 'twixt (between) me and him ; a waggon (carriage) had I, light, great-wheely, fully as it for our land-streets (country roads) was suitable ; in the pelt (fur coat) i-packed (wrapped), the instrument-case in the hand, stood I ride-ready (ready for the journey) on (in) the yard ; but the horse failed (was lacking), the horse . . .'

It will be evident from this how German and English have diverged from their common origin in respect of word-meanings or word-nuances. ' Stark ' means less ' strong ' in English than ' strongly plain ' ; ' waggon ' cannot mean a vehicle in general, as it still can in *Volkswagen*. ' I stand ' in German is *ich stehe* (' I stay ') ; ' I stood ' is *ich stand*. *Strasse* is like ' street ' but means a road as well as a town thoroughfare. *Dorf* (' village ') is a word in its own right, as well as a suffix in place-names (Düsseldorf), but ' thorp ' is only found in English in forms like Scunthorpe. *Pferd* has nothing to do with ' horse '. Still, the fact of kinship cannot be gainsaid, and there is fascination in looking for the family face under the whiskers.

FIVE

DAUGHTERS OF LATIN

Despite the closeness (and ultimate identity) of English and German, most British language-learners feel far more at home with the Romance sisters—French, Italian, Spanish, Portuguese. This may be a tribute to the beauty and hospitality of the Mediterranean countries, to the fact that they, unlike Germany, have done no real harm to Britain in the modern period, or, more likely, to the results of the Norman Conquest. William the Conqueror began the process of drawing English into the Latin family, and there is hardly a semanteme in the Romance languages which does not find a cognate word in English. In starting to learn French, Italian, or Spanish, we find ourselves already equipped with a vast number of words which, despite various phonetic disguises, bridge the distance between the lands of wine and the land of draught bitter.

It is interesting to see how English has entered into the Latin stream : it has dived into it both naked and wearing the clothes of Old French. For instance, the word ' count ' comes from the French *compter*, or its earlier form, and *compter* comes from Latin *computare*. But English itself has the word, directly taken from Latin, *compute*, whose meaning is perhaps a little more rarefied and intellectual than that of ' count '. Here are other examples :

Straight from French	*Straight from Latin*	*Latin*
conceit	concept	*conceptu*
constraint	constriction	*constrictione*
dainty	dignity	*dignitate*
esteem	estimate	*aestimare*
feat	fact	*facto*
loyal	legal	*legali*
poor	pauper	*pauperi*
royal	regal	*regali*
sure	secure	*securo*

(Those interested in the inflexions of Latin words will note that the

Latin ablative singular is given here : it was mainly from this form of the Latin noun that the Romance languages derived their own invariable noun-forms.)

English, then, absorbed many words direct from the French conqueror ; ever since, it has been taking words consciously and deliberately from classical Latin. It is not too much to say that any Latin semanteme (or meaning-word) is potentially an English word, and we are always at liberty to coin new Latinisms whenever we feel like it. Thus, if I want to talk about the farmer's wife of the ' Three Blind Mice ' round, I can—a little whimsically—refer to her as ' muricidal ' or ' mouse-killing '. The word may not be in the dictionary, but it is a true English word for all that. Language is, of course, a potential thing rather than a completed and fixed body of forms and words.

When I talk of ' classical Latin ', I am referring to a rather artificial, upper-class, literary kind of language, preserved in the work of Vergil, Horace, Cicero, and not generally used by the ordinary people of the Roman Empire.   For instance, the patrician or literary word for ' beautiful ' was *pulcher*, and we find this in the learned or facetious English word ' pulchritude '. But the common people used instead *bellus* (meaning, perhaps, ' pretty ') and this survives in the French *bel, beau, belle*, and the Italian *bello, bella*. As a spoken form, there are no derivatives of *pulcher*. *Formosus*, however, meaning perhaps ' shapely ' (' having form ') has become the Spanish word *hermoso*. The upper-class or literary word for a horse was *equus*, and this appears in various English words—' equine ', ' equestrian ', ' equerry ' (though in this last word there was a bit of mistaken etymology, *scutaria* perhaps being the Latin word from which it ultimately derived).   But the ordinary people called a horse *caballus*, from which has come the whole set of Romance words—French *cheval*, Spanish *caballo*, Italian *cavallo*. A gentleman—cavalier or *caballero*—is a man who rides a horse. Again, the upper-class Latin word ' to speak ' was *loqui* (a whole host of English words has come out of this), but the word in common use was *fabulari*. This produced French *parler*, Italian *parlare*, and Spanish *hablar*, as well as the contemptuous form once used in British colonies—' palaver '.

That, then, is our starting point : the Romance languages of to-day represent developments (involving a great deal of phonetic and semantic change) out of ' people's Latin '. Italian is, as it were, the domestic form that Latin took over the centuries ; Spanish and Portuguese are the

Latin taken to the Iberian peninsula ; French is the kind of Latin that was spoken in Paris and eventually became the tongue of the whole country. The essentially national terms now in use—we give the language the name of the people who speak it—took some time to come about. There was a time when a differentiation between the various kinds of spoken popular Latin was made in terms of the words for ' yes ' : there was *langue d'oc* in the French southern provinces ; *langue d'oïl* (*oïl* = *oui*) was spoken in the north ; *langue de sì* was Italian. This was as late as the end of the thirteenth century, very much a part of historical time. What we must do now is to show what happened to Latin in the various countries where it was spoken ; this will give us a bunch of keys for opening the four main boxes—French, Italian, Spanish, Portuguese. This book has no space for dealing with Rumanian or Catalan.

Let us look first at a number of English words derived directly from Latin : ' dictate ' (Latin *dicto*—' said ') ; ' fact (Latin *facto*—' done ') ; ' lactic ' (Latin *lacte*—' milk ') ; ' nocturnal ' (Latin *nocte*—' night ') ; ' October ' (Latin *octo*—' eight ' : October was, before Julius and Augustus Caesar added two extra months to the year, the eighth month). These all contain the consonants ' CT '. In Italian the Latin ' CT ' changed to ' TT ' ; in Spanish it became ' CH ' ; in Portuguese and French it appeared as ' IT ' :

Latin	Italian	Spanish	Portuguese	French
dicto	detto	dicho	dito	dit
facto	fatto	hecho	feito	fait
lacte	latte	leche	leite	lait
nocte	notte	noche	noite	nuit
octo	otto	ocho	oito	huit

Note how the Latin ablative singular ending is retained in Italian, Spanish, and Portuguese. French likes to rid its words of endings, and even what is retained in the spelling at the end of the word disappears in speech : none of the ' t 's here are pronounced.

Let us now take three Latin words which begin with consonant + L : *pleno*—' full ' (English ' plenitude ') ; *clave*—' key ' (English ' clavicle ', ' clavichord ') ; *flamma*—' flame '. In Italian the L becomes I :

pieno   *chiave* (the *ch* is pronounced /k/)   *fiamma*

F

In Spanish the three forms—PL ; CL ; FL—all become LL (the palatalised ' l ' somewhat like the ' lli ' of ' million ') :

    lleno   *llave*   *llama*

Portuguese also uses the one sound for the three Latin consonant-combinations :

    cheio   *chave*   *chama* (the *ch* is pronounced /ʃ/—' sh ')

French, as if to make up for dropping the Latin endings, retains the initial Latin consonants :

    plein   *clef*   *flamme*

To attempt to explain these changes, seemingly as capricious as the retentions, would require a great deal of speculation, bringing in questions of the influence of other tongues, for instance. But, a recurring motif in this book, the bilabial fricative /β/ has a lot to do with the following :

Latin	Italian	Spanish	Portuguese	French	English
capillo	*capello*	*cabello*	*cabelo*	*cheveu*	hair
lepore	*lepre*	*liebre*	*lebre*	*lièvre*	hare
sapere	*sapere*	*saber*	*saber*	*savoir*	to know
bibere	*bevere*	*beber*	*beber*	*buvoir*	to drink
habere	*avere*	*haber*	*haver*	*avoir*	to have

The *p*-between-vowels of Latin must have been very unsteady and wavering, and both the original and derived *b* must have had a fricative quality : only thus can we explain the present-day forms shown above, the French *v* a true ' v ' as in ' very ', the Spanish and Portuguese *b* with a soft ' buzzed ' quality suggesting /v/.

Let us look now at what has happened to some of the original Latin vowels :

Latin	Italian	Spanish	Portuguese	French	English
pede	*piede*	*pie*	*pé*	*pied*	foot
petra	*pietra*	*piedra*	*pedra*	*pierre*	stone
decem	*dieci*	*diez*	*dez*	*dix*	ten
morit	*muore*	*muere*	*morre*	*meurt*	(he) dies
potet	*può*	*puede*	*pode*	*peut*	(he) can
foco	*fuoco*	*fuego*	*fogo*	*feu*	fire

You will notice that the front vowel *e* is diphthongised in Italian,

Spanish, and French to *ie* (/ie/). The back vowel *o* has undergone three
different kinds of diphthongisation, though in French the *eu* that was
once *ue* has become a round front vowel—/ø/. The Italian *uo* merely
seems to emphasise that we are dealing with a very round sound ; the
Spanish *ue* shows a pushing-forward of the original Latin *o* to the front
of the mouth (/e/) and a preceding *u* to remind us that the changed
vowel was once a round one. The Latin double vowel AU has become
a simple vowel /o/ in the modern Romance tongues, though the spelling
does not always show this. Thus, the *auro* (' gold ') which we find in
English ' auriferous ' (' gold-bearing ') or even just in the chemical
symbol ' Au ', has become *oro* in Italian and Spanish, *ouro* (same
pronunciation /oro/) in Portuguese, and *or* in French. *Causa*, which we
find in English as ' cause ', has developed the meaning ' thing ' in the
Romance tongues, and appears as *cosa* in Italian and Spanish, *cousa*
in Portuguese, and *chose* in French.

It will be evident from all our examples so far that, of all the
daughters of Latin, French has strayed furthest away from home.
English words like ' scripture ', ' slave ', ' space ', ' spice ', and ' scald '
keep, in their initial sounds, very close to the original Latin, but see
what they have become in French : *écriture ; escalve ; espace ; épice ;
échauffer*. In general, the tendency of French is to get rid of an original
Latin *s* where possible. Sometimes it is guilty about this and erects
a circumflex as a kind of monument above the letter preceding the place
where the *s* used to be. Compare the following :

Middle French	*Modern French*	*English*
bastard	*bâtard*	bastard
beste	*bête*	beast
feste	*fête*	feast
oistre	*huître*	oyster

English, you will see, is far truer to the traditions of old French than is
modern French.

Another trick of French is to change the hard *c* of Latin (retained in
Italian, Spanish, and Portuguese) to *ch*. This means that a /k/ has been
pushed forward from the soft to the hard palate and turned into /ʃ/
(as in ' she ', ' ship '). English has, incidentally, done the same thing
with a few Latin words, so that *episcopus* appears as ' bishop ' and
casius became ' cheese '. But French is fairly consistent :

F*

Latin	French	English
caballo	cheval	horse
capra	chèvre	goat
caro	cher	dear
cantare	chanter	to sing
capitulo	chapitre	chapter

The voiced velar consonant of Latin—/g/—has been treated even more harshly than /k/ when it appears in the middle of a Latin word : *Augusto* (' August ') has become *Août* (pronounced /u/) ; *lege* (' law ') appears as *loi ; nigro* (' black ') is Frenchified to *noir*. Elimination, shortening, has been really drastic in French : consider that *eau* (/o/) comes from *aqua* (' water '), and that *Noël* (' Christmas ') derives ultimately from *Natalis* (' natal ', ' relating to birth '). The paring-down is, of course, often really more drastic than it looks, so that *front* (' forehead '), though its spelling shows it to be derived from Latin *fronte*, no longer has an articulated *t*, and the *n* has been diminished to a mere snorting of the preceding vowel. *Front*, then, is pronounced /frɔ̃/.

Spanish and Portuguese show their own patterns of divergence— both singly and (as the two main ' Iberian languages ') collectively. But both look more like Latin than does French. What gives Spanish its piquancy is its traces of the influence of non-Indo-European languages. The Basque tongue has no /f/, and this seems reflected in the following :

Latin	Spanish	English
fabulari	hablar	to speak
facere	hacer	to make
filio	hijo	son
folia	hoja	leaf

The *h* has no sound here, nor, indeed, in any of the Romance languages, though it seems to have had its full aspirate value in Latin. Note that the middle *l* of the last two Latin words on the above list has become *j*—pronounced /x/, the ' ch ' of ' loch '—in Spanish. The inevitable Arabic influence on Spanish is mainly one of vocabulary, giving words like *mezquino* (' poor '), *alguacil* (' constable '), *aljibe* (' cistern '), *laúd* (' lute '), *ataúd* (' coffin ').

Portuguese resembles French in having eliminated some of the nasals of original Latin and substituted nasalisation of the preceding vowel, or even (unlike French) diphthong. Spanish *lana* (' wool ') appears in Portuguese as *lã*; Spanish *pan* (' bread ') becomes Portuguese *pão*. And Portuguese, somewhat like Italian, is not always concerned about retaining an original Latin ' L '. Latin *caelum* (' sky ') appears in French as *ciel* and in Spanish as *cielo*; but Portuguese has *céu*. Latin and Italian *volare* (' to fly ') is *volar* in Spanish but *voar* in Portuguese. The ' L ' has even disappeared in the definite articles, so that *lo* and *la* have become *o* and *a*. Occasionally Portuguese has *r* where other Romance tongues have *l*: what is *blanc* in French, *bianco* in Italian, and *blanco* in Spanish is *branco* in Portuguese. One is not ' much obliged ' in Portugal; one is *muito obrigado*.

When we have considered all the sound-shifts, distortions, and disguises that make the modern Romance languages different from Latin and from the Latin part of English, we are still left with a corpus of transparent identities. If English ' experience ' is *experiencia* in Spanish, *experiência* in Portuguese, and *experienza* in Italian, we should have no difficulty in rendering ' impudence ', ' indifference ', and so on in those languages. Similarly, the ending ' -ment ' in ' argument ', ' monument ', ' element ' will meet *-mento* in all three. The suffix ' -ty ' in ' identity ' corresponds to French *-té*, Spanish *-dad*, Portuguese *-dade*, and Italian *-tà*. And words like ' education ' appear as French *éducation*, Spanish *educación*, Portuguese *educação*, and Italian *educazione*. The recognition that our own language is, to some extent, as much a child of the Roman Empire as the true full-blooded Latin tongues of to-day should encourage us in our work on them. We may even eventually take breath and plunge into Rumanian, which has developed from the language spoken by Trajan's soldiers in the province of Dacia. There we shall find that the strange-looking *omul* is really *homo ille* (' the man '), and *lupul* is *lupus ille* (' the wolf '). Part of the pleasure of language-learning is the search for hidden identities.

Every schoolboy knows that the Latin verb is a nightmare. The nightmare has partly dispersed in the descendants of Latin, which still, nevertheless, make heavier going of verbs than English or German. But we ought to remember that the common people of the Roman Empire were already at work on a simplification and rationalisation which did not appeal to the patrician writers and their readers, and that this has left its mark on the modern Latin languages. Where Cicero or Vergil would write *amavi* for ' I have loved ', the Roman plebs would prefer a form like our own : *habeo* (I have) *amatum* (loved). In all the Romance languages you can make a past form, a future, and a conditional out of the verb ' to have ', and this makes the learning of this verb an important—and not very difficult—task. Thus, the French *j'ai*—' I have '—gives us the conversational past tense of *j'ai aimé* (' I (have) loved ') and the future *j'aimerai* (infinitive *aimer* + *ai*). The past tense (imperfect) *j'avais*—' I had '—will give not only the pluperfect ' I had loved '—*j'avais aimé*—but the conditional ' I would (might love '—*j'aimerais* (infinitive *aimer* + *-ais*). The same process will be found in the sister languages of French.

Enough, perhaps, has been said in this chapter to indicate possible lines of study, the key-maxim being ' search for likenesses to English, identities in all languages of the group '. Ideally, one should know one Romance language really well, have a reading knowledge of the others, and be willing to acquire a conversational knowledge of any of those at, say, six weeks' notice.

SIX

PIERCING THE IRON CURTAIN

RUSSIAN is as rich and satisfying as Christmas pudding, but what tends to dull the appetite for learning it is the apparent difficulty of the alphabet. I say 'apparent' advisedly, for it can be mastered in an hour or so. Once learnt, it will be seen as entirely suitable for the language it clothes, and Romanisation only makes Russian look clumsy. Compare the following :

Хрущёв

Kh r u shch e v

(The final consonant is unvoiced to /f/. Russian, like German, tends to unvoice its end-sounds.)

The following geographical names are useful for learning Cyrillic script :

Африка	Afrika	Africa
Брюссель	Briussel'	Brussels
Кембридж	Kyembridzh	Cambridge
Голландия	Gollandiya	Holland
Вальпарайзо	Val'paraizo	Valparaiso
Мельбурн	Myel'burn	Melbourne
Цейлон	Tsyeilon	Ceylon

Corresponding to the apostrophe in the second column above, you will notice the symbol ь, which puzzles most learners of Russian. It indicates that the preceding consonant is palatalised—that is, pulled from its normal mouth-position on to the hard palate. The difference between л (/l/) and ль (/λ/) is close to the difference between the 'l' of 'mill' and the 'lli' of 'million'. Any consonant which has this 'softening' symbol after it is, as it were, prevented from being exploded in the usual way : a 'y' (as in 'yes') comes along and chokes it.

The difference between a plain consonant and a palatalised one is not (as is the difference between dark and clear L in English) allophonic.

The addition of ь makes a new phoneme, as is shown by the difference in meaning between the following :

угол — corner	уголь — coal
брат — brother	брать — to take

Palatalisation is dear to the heart of Russian, and there is a perfect opposition of plain and palatalised vowels :

А, а as in ' h*a*rd '	Я, я as in ' *y*ard '
Э, э as in ' d*e*n '	Е, е as in ' *ye*s '
О, о as in ' *o*n '	Ё, ё as in ' *yo*nder '
У, у as in ' bl*ue* '	Ю, ю as in ' *you* '

One Russian vowel which seems to have no equivalent in any other language is represented by ы. It is very much like the English /ɪ/ in ' sit ', ' fit ', but more centralised (properly /ɨ/) and sometimes pronounced with lip-rounding. For the rest, the Russian sound-system is straightforward enough, and Russian, like English, is willing to ' weaken ' a vowel if it is not in a stressed position. Thus, *Doktor Zhivago* does not, as would be the case in a Romance language, preserve the rounded final *o*. The vowel is unstressed and becomes something like *a*.

The learning of stress in Russian is difficult : there are no stress-rules, and one is reminded again of English. But most Russian primers put a stress-diacritic (′) above the stressed vowel of a word, and this helps. Stress is vigorous, emphasising the very Indo-European nature of the language. The stressed vowel of the word, phrase or sentence takes up so much vocalic energy that none of the other vowels carry anything like their full quality. The tone of Russian is virile, suggesting that the sounds are pushed back into the throat rather than, as with French or Italian, placed in the front of the mouth. There is a grumbling bearish quality about a good deal of Russian speech.

Russian has plenty of grammar but, to anyone who has studied a classical Indo-European language like Latin, there will not seem to be anything unfamiliar. There are three genders, words ending in a consonant or the semi-vowel й (/j/) tending to masculinity, feminine words being, as with the Romance tongues, those with an -*a* or -*ya* ending, and neuter nouns terminating in -*o* or -*ye*. Adjectives (which come before the noun) have similar endings, and both adjectives and nouns have full batteries of inflexions.

The endings of the various parts of the verb have a Latin flavour. ' I read ' is *ya chitáyu,* ' he reads ' is *on chitáyet,* ' we read ' is *mi* (мы) *chitáyem,* and ' they read ' is *oni chitáyut.* There is only one past tense, but its endings reflect the gender of the subject, so that ' I read ' (/rɛd/) or ' I have read ' will be *ya chitál, ya chitála,* or *ya chitálo* according to the gender of the speaker. The other persons of the singular (' thou ', ' he, she, it ') take the same endings as does *ya,* and the plural— whether ' we ', ' you ', or ' they '—has the invariable ending *-i* (*mi chitáli*—' we read ' ; *oní chitáli*—' they read ', where ' read ' = /rɛd/).

The Russian verb has only three tenses, while English has twelve. To make up for this deficiency, Russian introduces what are called ' aspects of the verb '—the *imperfective* and the *perfective.* If *chitál* means ' I have read ', the addition of a prefix will produce *prochitál*— ' I have finished reading ' ; *budu chitat'* (the apostrophe indicates ь) means ' I shall read ', but *prochitáyu* (a present tense form used with a future meaning) will mean ' I shall read (it) through '. The simple form of the verb, then, implies no completion of action and hence is imperfective ; the prefix changes it to a perfective form or aspect, and completion of the action is the very essence of its meaning. Here are other examples :

Ya rabótayu—I work (continuously, habitually, or recurrently)

Ya porabótal—I did some work (i.e. completed some)

Ya porabótayu—I shall do some (a little) work (a present tense cannot indicate completion, so the present-tense form of perfective verbs has to convey a future meaning).

The bulk of the Russian vocabulary is pure Slavonic, but a vast number of loan-words (from Latin, German, French, even English) helps our learning task :

abort—abortion, miscarriage
abstraktniy—abstract
absurd—absurdity
ambitsiya—ambition
arka—arch
armiya—army
banknota—bank-note

bryesh'—breach, gap
bufyet—sideboard, buffet
vokal'niy—vocal
geroy—hero
gimn—hymn
dyek—deck
diplomaticheskiy—diplomatic
direktor—director, manager, chief
evangelist—evangelist
zal—hall (cf. French *salle*)
idyot—idiot
identichniy—identical
instruktsiya—instruction
kanal'ya—rogue, rascal (cf. French *canaille*, Italian *canaglia*)
karta—card, map, menu
katar—catarrh
konfyeta—sweetmeat
korpus—body, army corps
korrektniy—correct, proper
korryespondyentsya—correspondence
kortezh—procession, cortège
langust—lobster (cf. French *langouste*)
marsh—march
marshrut—itinerary, route-march
maskarad—fancy-dress ball
planyeta—planet
plug—plough
tabak—tobacco
talya—waist (cf. French *taille*)
tambur—drum (cf. French *tambour*)
tramvay—tram, tramway
tsyellyulyaniy—cellular
sharlatan—charlatan
shofyor—chauffeur

It is time to look at a little Russian in action, and we cannot do better than take a short poem by Pushkin, the Byron of Russian literature. Here it is, first, in Cyrillic script :

Я вас люби́л ; любо́вь ещё, быть-мо́жет,
В душе́ мое́й уга́сла не совсе́м ;
Но пусть она́ вас бо́льше не трево́жит ;
Я не хочу́ печа́лить вас ниче́м.
Я вас люби́л безмо́лвно, безнадёжно,
То ра́достью, то ре́вностью томи́м ;
Я вас люби́л так и́скренно, так не́жно,
Как дай вам Бог люби́мой бы́ть други́м.

And here is an attempt at transliteration into the Roman alphabet :

Ya vas lyubil ; lyubov' yeshcho, bit'-mozhet,
V dushe moyey ugasla nye sovsyem ;
No pust' ona vas bol'she nye tryevozhit ;
Ya nye khochu pyechalit' vas nichem.
Ya vas lyubil byezmolvno, byeznadyozhno,
To radost'yu, to revnost'yu tomim ;
Ya vas lyubil tak iskryenno, tak nyezhno,
Kak day vam Bog lyubimoy bit' drugim.

(Vowels have their ' Continental ' values ; ' y ' always stands for the sound in ' yes ' ; ' g ' is always hard, as in ' got ' ; the apostrophe stands for the softener or palataliser ь).

The key-words are *Ya vas lyubil* (literally, ' I you loved '). Let us keep to the Russian word-order for our literal translation : ' I you loved ; love still, perhaps/in spirit my has-been-extinguished (*ugasla*) not entirely ;/but it you more let not trouble (let it trouble you no more) ; /I not wish to sadden you with nothing./I you loved without-(*byez*)-utterance (silently), without-hope (hopelessly),/now from joy, now from jealousy languishing ;/I you loved so sincerely, so tenderly,/ as grant you God be loved by another.'

Russian has a huge and important literature which cries out to be read (even with the aid of a crib) in the original.

F**

SEVEN

MALAY

WE have taken brief tastes of Indo-European languages and seen what they have in common—inflexions, conjugations, genders, and certain words. It will be salutary for us to move outside the great family and examine briefly one of the languages of the East. I choose Malay because of its interest and its importance. It is a lingua franca for South-East Asia and, as *Bahasa* (literally, ' The Language '), it is the national tongue of Indonesia. It is rich in dialects and cognate with the languages of the Dayaks and Ibans in Borneo, as well as (though more remotely) with Fijian and Maori, so it will be met in many forms. The Federation of Malaya accepts the dialect of Johore as its national language (the language of government announcements and official literature), and this is close enough to President Soekarno's *Bahasa*. The Muslim invaders of Malacca gave Malay a form of the Arabic alphabet (called the *Jawi* or ' Eastern ' form), but Romanisation has proved easy. Dutch Romanisation differs from British, as it follows the spelling conventions of the Dutch language. Thus, the word for ' grandchild ' is spelt *tjoetjoe* in *Bahasa*, but *chuchu* in Malayan Malay. We shall, naturally, keep to British Romanisation, not because it is British, but because its symbols hold close to the main European alphabetic stream.

Malay has no frightening phonetic curiosities. Final plosives like /t/, /d/, /p/, /b/ are initiated but not completed, and the letter ' k ' stands for a glottal stop in words like *anak* (' child '), *sĕjuk* (cold), *itek* (' duck '). Words can begin with /ŋ/ (as in ' sing ', ' song ', ' thing '), something unheard of in Indo-European languages. The vowel symbols have roughly the same value as in Italian, but ' ĕ ' stands for the neutral /ə/ of the second syllable in ' father ', ' brother ', ' mother '. There is a tendency for final *a* in a word like *ada* (' there is ', ' there are ') to be pronounced like the vowel of French *bleu*. Stress is either non-existent or too light to be important. Articulation is gentle and rapid. Malay is at the opposite pole to Russian and German : it is not a ponderous language.

What strikes the learner of Malay is the complete lack of those typically Indo-European properties—gender, inflection, conjugation. It is like diving into a bath of pure logic. Everything is pared to a minimum. Let us first look at the pronouns. *Saya* can be ' I ', ' me ', or, in postposition, ' my '. Thus ' I hit him ' is *saya pukul dia* ; ' he hits me ' is *dia pukul saya* ; ' my wife ' is *istĕri saya*. *Dia*, as you will see, is as invariable as *saya*, and it can stand for ' he ', ' she ', or ' it ' ; in speech it can also mean ' they ', the highbrow *mĕreka* being reserved for the written form of the language. ' His wife ' can be *istĕri dia*, but *istĕri-nya* is perhaps preferred, that nasalisation of *di-* to *ny-* forming an interesting parallel to Welsh. The Malay word for *you* is slippery and variable, showing the influence of old taboos : it is as though there is something dangerous in using a second-person pronoun. And so a Malay will choose carefully in asking the question ' What do you want ? ' To a person of superior social status he will say *Apa tuan mahu* ? (' What does the gentleman want ? ') or perhaps *Apa ĕnche mahu* ? (slightly lower social status). There are other words which might be used : *lu* for a Chinese, *tuanku* (' my lord ') to a ruler, *tĕngku* and *ĕngku* for rajas, *dato'* for chiefs, *'che guru* for a schoolmaster, and forms like *mika, awak, ĕngkau* among equals and near-equals. It is a difficult and touchy business, this choice of the right word for ' you ', and offence can easily be taken. Malay has one advantage over the Indo-European tongues in its words for ' we ' : *kami* can exclude the person addressed, *kita* includes him. In Borneo *kita* is used for ' you ', so that one has a sort of governess flavour in statements like ' We mustn't do that again, must we ? '

The noun is invariable, and does not even need to change in the plural. *Rokok* is ' cigarette ', ' a cigarette ', ' the cigarette ', or ' cigarettes ', the context making all clear. Pluralisation is often shown by duplication, but *rokok-rokok* (written as *rokok2*) implies a variety, different kinds of cigarettes, rather than a straight plural. When number is specified— ' two cigarettes '—or the nature of the pluralisation is significant, as in ' many cigarettes ', a very Eastern device is used (it is also found in Chinese). This is the ' numerical coefficient ', and it varies according to the semantic nature of the noun involved. Human beings are preceded by the announcement ' human being ', so that ' two clerks ' is *dua orang kĕrani*, ' four soldiers ' is *ĕmpat orang soldadu* (note the Portuguese loan-word *soldadu*, a relic of Portuguese Malacca), and ' many women ' is *banyak orang pĕrĕmpuan*. The numerical coefficient for animals is *ekor*—'tail '—and ' ten cats ' is hence *sa-puloh ekor kuching*. Subtlety is required for inanimate objects. For instance, anything big, bulky, round has the coefficient *buah* (literally ' fruit ') : ' a car ' is *sa-buah kĕreta* and ' five hundred houses ' is *lima ratus buah rumah*.

If one digs deeply enough into Malay, one comes to the conclusion that the Western concept of ' parts of speech ' is alien to it. A word is a word is a word, and it can be used as any part of a syntactical pattern. Thus, *makan* expresses the notion of food, eating, and *makan saya* can, logically, mean either ' eat me ' or ' my food '. *Tari* is either ' dance ' (the noun), the idea of dancing, or the active verb ' to dance '. But, especially in written Malay, there is an interesting battery of suffixes and prefixes to call on which make more specific the function of the word in question. So *tarian* can only mean ' a dance ' or ' the dance ', while *mĕnari* (again the Welsh-type nasal mutation) has to be a verb. Much can be made out of little. The word *ada* means any of the following (I quote from Wilkinson's admirable Malay–English dictionary) : ' to be present, to exist, to be at home (to a visitor), to exist in connection with, to appertain to, to have.' The root meaning is ' existence '. *Adakan* or *mĕngadakan* (the suffix *-kan* having a causative function) means ' to call into existence, to appoint '. *Bĕrada* is a polite way of saying ' to be present ', but *orang yang bĕrada* means ' people of standing '. *Kĕadaan* (noun-suffix *-an*, abstract-noun-prefix *kĕ-*) means ' state, existence, condition of life, position '. One prefix, *tĕr-*, adds a remarkable nuance to a verb. If *kilat* has the primary meaning of ' a flash (of lightning) ', and *bĕrkilat* means ' to flash ', *tĕrkilat* means ' to flash suddenly, unawares ', as of a darting fish.

Malay has certain words which cannot be assigned to any Western category. A good example is *pun*, literally untranslatable. It is an emphasising word, a word that ' lights up ' the semanteme that goes before : *itu pun* means ' that also '; *sakali pun* is something like ' yet '; *dia pun pĕrgi* means ' he also went ', the *pun* bestowing a past meaning on the invariable verb-form *pĕrgi*. There is no single meaning for *pun*, and it is hard to get at its roots and origin ; its correct use is incredibly difficult to learn. The enclitic *-lah* is again untranslatable : it lends force to what goes before, so that *orang itu-lah yang pĕrgi* means ' It was *that* person who went '. Words like these are perhaps essential to a language that does not use vocal stress for emphasis.

The vocabulary of Malay is, in its fundamentals, entirely fitted to the needs of a people concerned with the concrete processes of everyday living—fishing, gathering fruit and coconuts, begetting children, lying in the sun. This makes it poetical, metaphorical, happier with proverbs than with abstract constatations. But the Arabs brought Islam and the religious and philosophical terms that go with it ; loan-words from Portuguese and English are numerous ; the need to cope—in education, newspapers, government directives—with the intellectual notions of the modern world has forced Malay scholars, teachers, and editors to fashion neologisms—usually out of Arabic or (and India has had its influence, too) Sanskrit. There have to be trade unions, strikes, parent-teacher associations, co-operative societies. A new world of words, bewildering to the peasant, is being forged.

Whether Malay can be democratised is another matter. The feudal structure of Malay society has had a remarkable effect on the language. Words appropriate to the common man cannot be used in connection with a ruler—sultan or raja. I walk (*jalan kaki*—' go with foot ') but the Sultan must *běrangkat*. I eat (*makan*), but the Sultan *santap*. I sleep (*tidor*), while the Sultan *běradu*. This may seem a lot of un-necessary luggage (there are, of course, many other specifically ' royal ' words), and, similarly, one is sometimes impatient at the unwillingness of Malay to *generalise* (there is no one word for ' you ' ; ' rice ' is *padi* when growing, *běras* in the shops, *nasi* on the table ; there is no single word for ' brother ' or for ' sister '). But there is a fine economy and logic in the accidence and syntax of the language, just as there is in the numerical system. Malay starts its ' teens ' at eleven (*sa-bělas* = 11 ; *duabělas* = 12 ; *tigabělas* = 13, and so on) and wonders why the West counts as though it had twelve fingers. The fact is that there is no occasion for the philologists of Europe to ' look down ' on Malay as a primitive and outlandish language : it has solved linguistic problems that bother the speaker of English, German, or French ; it has achieved a logic and simplicity which the Western tongues do not know. Every school curriculum in Europe should provide an opportunity for at least a dabbling examination of an Oriental language, in order to see how the other half of the world (very much more than a half) contrives not only to live but to think and express itself.

We shall end with two specimens of Malay writing, the first a poem. A popular Malay verse-form is the *pantun*, a quatrain which presents

two contrasted ideas (two lines to each) which are made to show a kinship through similarity of sound. It is a subtle form, in which
expression—as in all true art—matters more than content. Every
Malay has a great store of *pantuns* in his memory ; some Malays are
adept at improvising them. Here is one of the loveliest of the traditional
pantuns, known everywhere in South-East Asia :

> *Kalau tuan mudek ka-hulu,*
> *Charikan saya bunga kĕmoja.*
> *Kalau tuan mati dahulu,*
> *Nantikan saya di-pintu shurga.*

This means literally : ' If lord travel to-riverhead,/Look for me for
flower frangipanni./If lord die first (before),/Wait for me at-gate
heaven.' A freer translation would be : ' If you, my lover, go up-river,
find me some frangipanni. Should you be the first of us two to die, wait
for me at the gates of heaven.' Note the way in which the first and
third lines, and the second and fourth lines, chime in assonance. Let us
now look at the component words :

Kalau   if (met also as *jikalau* and *jika*).

tuan   literally ' master ', ' lord ', ' lady '. Used by a lover to his
        mistress, or vice versa.

mudek   an invariable verb-form whose meaning is ' travelling up-
        stream '. Malay is particular about the right word, hating
        to generalise with some such colourless form as *pĕrgi*—
        ' to go '.

ka-   to, towards, into.

hulu   the root meaning is ' head, upper portion '. An ordinary
        person has a *kĕpala* under his hat, but a royal personage
        has a *hulu*. *Hulu* can be the hilt of a weapon (*hulu kĕris*).
        With the addition of the noun-prefix *pĕ-* and a linking
        nasal we get *pĕnghulu*—' headman of a village '. Here
        hulu means ' head of the river '.

Charikan   the root is *chari*—' searching '—and the addition of *-kan*
        makes the verb ' to search for anything '.

saya   I, me, for me, etc.

bunga   flower.

kĕmoja   frangipanni (*kĕmboja* is another form). Like the cypress of
        the West, frangipanni is associated with graveyards.

mati   death, dying, to die.

dahulu   before, past, ahead of time.

Nantikan   *nanti* means ' waiting ' (it sometimes means ' shall ', ' will ',
             and thus acts as a future auxiliary). Here the suffix -*kan*
             gives us the specific verb ' to wait for '.

di-   in, on, at.

pintu   door, gate.

shurga   (a Sanskrit loan-word) heaven.

Now let us examine a brief piece of modern Malay prose. It is taken
from the introduction to *Pělita Bahasa Mělayu*—literally, ' Lamp of the
Malay Language '—by Za'ba (an illustrious name in Malaya but hardly
known here). Its theme is appropriate to this book on language in
general :

Tiap-tiap (each, every) *bahasa* (language) *yang* (which) *hidup* (alive,
living) *memang* (naturally, as a matter of course) *tabi'at* (character,
nature) *dan* (and) *adat nya* (behaviour-its) *tumboh* (sprout, spring up,
erupt) *dan bĕrtambah* (increase, grow, develop) *sĕrta* (with, together
with) *bĕrubah* (being altered) *pĕrlahan-lahan* (slowly) *dari* (from) *suatu*
(one) *masa* (time) *ka-* (to) *suatu masa ; jika* (if) *tiada* (there is not)
tumboh atau (or) *bĕrtambah dan bĕrubah maka* (an untranslatable
' punctuation word ' signifying the end of a subordinate clause)
ĕrti-nya (literally, the meaning of it = that is to say) *tiada bĕrgĕrak,*
(to move, to stir) *dan tiada bĕrgĕrak itu* (that) *ĕrti-nya* ' *mati* ' (dead)
sa-bagaimana (in the same way as) *bahasa Sanskrit dan Latin tĕlah*
(have) *mati* (died).

Here is a free translation :

' The character and usage of any language which is living grow and
develop—in a perfectly natural way—and change slowly with the
passage of time ; if there were no growth and development and change,
then the language would be static, and when a language is static that
language has died, just as the Sanskrit and Latin tongues have died.'

Look at the Malay once more :

*Tiap-tiap bahasa yang hidup memang tabi'at dan adat-nya tumboh dan
bĕrtambah sĕrta bĕrubah pĕrlahan-lahan dari suatu masa ka-suatu masa ;
jika tiada tumboh atau bĕrtambah dan bĕrubah maka ĕrti-nya tiada*

bĕrgĕrak, dan tiada bĕrgĕrak itu ĕrtinya ' mati' sa-bagaimana bahasa Sanskrit dan Latin tĕlah mati.

It is evidently a fine, subtle, musical language, flavoursome with its duplications and repetitions. I have been haunted for many years by a phrase from an old Malay history, one which seems to sum up the suggestive possibilities of the language : *lima ratus orang orang pĕrang*—' five hundred fighting men '. Could any language do better ?

EIGHT

THE BREAKING OF BABEL

THE fact that the human race speaks many languages—most of them mutually unintelligible—has traditionally been regarded as a curse. The myth of Babel and the divine confusion of tongues converts an age-long process into a sudden and quite unexpected catastrophe. The ' unscrambling ' of linguistic chaos is celebrated at Pentecost, one of the great feasts of the Church calendar. Quite outside the realms of myth and miracle, is it possible for man to redeem the curse, to create or choose a common language for the whole of the civilised world ?

Certain men have thought so, and their thoughts have tended to run on the same lines : let every man be bilingual, with his first language his own regional mother-tongue, his second language a world auxiliary ; let this world auxiliary be an artificial language, for only an artificial language can be truly supranational. One can see the point well enough : an existing language, like English or French or Spanish, is bound to have nationalistic associations unpleasing to all but its native speakers, and so it is not really suitable as a world auxiliary language. Hence—so the argument runs—the need for a sort of plastic language, something as neutral and aseptic as polythene.

Various artificial languages have, in fact, been painfully manufactured and some of them are—though not on a world scale—in periodic use. Volapük was the first (1880—the creation of J. M. Schleyer, a German priest) and it swiftly died out because it was too complicated : a Malay would have fainted at the needless luggage of inflexions. From it we can learn how difficult it is for a language-maker to shed inborn prejudices : the messy grammar, the huge portmanteau-words of German, seemed natural to Schleyer, and he incorporated them accordingly in his brain-child. Volapük was logical (there were no irregular verbs, no exceptions to rules of noun-inflexion) but it was not simple. It took a long time for auxiliary-makers to learn how little grammar languages like Malay, Persian, and Chinese (and, for that matter, English) really require. Why should one have to slave over masses of grammar in one's world auxiliary when grammar hardly exists in one's mother-tongue ? Schleyer could not see this.

1887 saw the birth of Esperanto, perhaps still the most popular of the artificial auxiliaries. Its creator, Dr Zamenhof, a Russian-Polish Jew, presented it as *Linguo Internacia de la Doktoro Esperanto*, this latter pseudonym meaning ' hopeful ', and the name has stuck. Zamenhof saw that the great need was to have as little grammar as possible and he realised, from his studies of English, how unfunctional most grammar was. But he insists on an accusative case (*Ni lernas Esperanton*— ' we're learning Esperanto ') and the agreement of adjective and noun. His vocabulary is eclectic—in other words, he draws from all the big European languages in fair proportion ; what he does not do, however, is to remember how many international words already exist in those languages. If Latin has, for ' school ', the word *schola*, and Swedish has *skola*, German *Schule*, Italian *scuola*, and even Malay *sĕkolah*, one is entitled to expect something like *skol* or *scolo* or *skula* in an international auxiliary. But Esperanto has *lernejo*.

Other man-made languages have followed Esperanto—Ido and Esperantido (simplifications of Esperanto), Interlingua (a kind of Latin without Latin grammar), Novial (a hybrid creation of the great philologist Otto Jespersen), Interglossa (a language very sensibly contrived out of Greek roots—Greek being our international scientific language—by Lancelot Hogben). But we tend to return, in our search for a bomb for Babel, to existing tongues. French has long been an international language of diplomacy and culture, ecumenical councils carry on in Church Latin. Now, more and more, it is evident that English will prove the great international tongue for all kinds of communication—not purely ambassadorial or ecclesiastical.

There are extrinsic reasons for the spread of English, and these are sufficiently well known. The English have long been a maritime people, concerned with exporting not only goods in their ships but also English-speaking communities. Of these America has become the most powerful, leader of the so-called Free World. Meanwhile, there remains a loosely-linked commonwealth in which English is either the first language or the chief auxiliary. Advances in technology have been associated with English, and so has air communication between countries and continents : English is the language of international pilots. For a Dutch, Indian, or Chinese child, the first lessons in English already represent a key to the whole of the outside world, not merely the American or British part of it.

But there are certain intrinsic elements in English which render it suitable as an international auxiliary. It has far less unnecessary grammar than any other Indo-European tongue (with the exception of Persian); it has a considerable Graeco-Latin vocabulary, itself international; it can be polysyllabic, like Russian or German or Finnish, or monosyllabic, like Chinese. It has made its way, with no deliberate pushing, in the great world; it is felt that, with certain adaptations and deliberate simplifications, it can go still further.

This was the view of C. K. Ogden and I. A. Richards, the devisers of Basic English. In their *The Meaning of Meaning* they asked a fundamental question : what is the absolute minimum of English words required to define all the words in a dictionary ? They came to the conclusion that it was something like 800. It seemed possible, then, to make out of English a very simple auxiliary, one that could be learned in two or three months. They proved, by a number of translations, that the most monumental work of English literature could be rendered accurately—though with an inevitable loss of ' magic '—into Basic, and that the average reader would be unaware of anything strange, forced, or insufficient.

The suitability of English for this reducing treatment is exemplified in its peculiar aptitude for verb-making. For instance, the colourless word ' get ' can, in combination with various helper-words, do a remarkable number of jobs : ' I got to bed late but got up quite early, got my clothes on, got some breakfast, got on the bus, and got to the office on time. I got my ledgers out and got down to work, got a cup of coffee at eleven and got out to lunch at twelve-thirty. (I always get a good cheap lunch in the ABC.) I got back to the office at two and got away at five-thirty, got home safely, got my tea, then got out to the pub as quickly as possible : some friends and I were having a get-together . . .' Words like ' go ' and ' put ' show equal versatility. Meat can ' go off ' in hot weather ; when a woman nags she ' goes on and on and on ' at her husband ; if we like something, we say we ' go for it '. One ' puts up ' with adversity, ' puts up ' somebody for the night or for club membership ; a vicious dog may be ' put down ' by the vet ; you ' put in ' a good word for somebody. A language like French cannot say ' go up ' or ' go down ', only *ascendre* or *déscendre*.

Teachers of English to foreigners are sometimes shy of the various 'get' combinations, chiefly because they have long—though foolishly—been considered vulgar or 'unliterary'. It is still regarded, in examination-setting circles, as more decent to 'propose' a new member than to 'put him up', to 'quell' a rebellion rather than 'put it down'. Thus, the huge advantages that the 'synthetising' powers of English have for the foreign student are snobbishly pushed into a dusty cupboard.

But, before English can be stripped to the bone and turned into a real world auxiliary, the academic pundits will have to learn a little more more about practical semantics ; they will have to submit to (or put up with) the most outrageous rationalisations. All verbs will have to become weak, forms like 'I swimmed' and 'I have swimmed' being semantically clear and hence throughly admissible. Verb-inflexions must go : if 'I must'/'he must' is accepted, then no noses may be wrinkled at 'I go'/'he go' (nor, of course, at 'I goed'). This process of simplification is, of course, regularly at work with uneducated foreign speakers of English ; it is something, alas, that British children have to unlearn, along with 'mouse'/'mouses' and 'foot'/'foots'.

When Basic English first appeared, some people assumed that Ogden and Richards's proposal was to replace orthodox English with this new and simpler form. But such a thing, even if possible, could never be regarded by any sensible person as desirable. With our first language, we move in the direction of ever greater subtlety of distinction in meaning, sharpening the instruments for ever deeper probings into thought, emotion, and motivation ; with an auxiliary, our aim is to achieve a contact—however minimal—with foreign minds. A foreigner learning some such simple type of English as Basic would not be precluded from using that as a way into 'total English'. It would be possible for the two—Basic and Total—to be used side by side as the various forms of the 'contact vernacular' known as Pidgin English ('pidgin' being a corruption of 'business') are used by Englishmen in contact with natives of New Guinea and the African ports. English has room, and has made room, for a large number of overseas English dialects, as the new and flourishing literatures of British Africa and the Caribbean clearly show.

What tends to happen to English, however, when spoken in foreign territories, is that it is absorbed too thoroughly, ceases to be an outward-looking auxiliary and becomes a mere dialect of the mother-tongue. This is certainly true of some of the communities of India, especially where the mother-tongue does not belong to the Indo-European family : Tamils, who speak a Dravidian language, are adept at turning English into a Tamil dialect—the phonemes, idioms, pace being so thoroughly Tamilised, that it is not possible for a non-Tamil English-speaker to understand very well. Writing and reading are, of course, a different matter. I could make no sense out of *bu lokkar* until it was written down for me as ' bullock cart '.

We have to reconcile ourselves to hard linguistic facts. Languages will always change, whatever we try to do about it, and out of local changes come local languages. English is already changing into new languages in various parts of the world, mutually unintelligible, unintelligible to the English-born. English—full of unstable diphthongs and vowels, carrying a stress-system not always properly understood—lends itself far more to change than does a language like Italian, whose simple vowels have hardly altered in 2,000 years. But, if there is a confusion of English-speaking tongues, the written word remains constant enough, unifying as the ideograms of Chinese unify. And English is big enough to enclose any number of aberrations.

NINE

THE FUTURE OF ENGLISH

WE have already considered very briefly what part English is likely to play as a world auxiliary. It remains for us to illustrate one of our main themes, that of the changeability of language in general, by reference to what seems to be happening to English in those countries where it is a first language, and what will probably happen in the future.

Linguistic change is something so gradual that we barely notice it, though occasionally we will wake up to a sudden realisation that a new word or phrase, formerly unknown, is in general use, or that a form that was once ' wrong ' has become ' right '. At school we were taught that ' owing to ' and ' due to ' are not interchangeable, that ' owing to ' may begin a phrase but ' due to ' only be used after the verb ' to be '. But British Railways have printed thousands of posters announcing : ' Due to adverse weather conditions trains may be late.' What was once a solecism is now evidently acceptable : one hears ' due to ' as a conjunctive phrase not only on the Independent Television News but also on the BBC—once a stronghold of linguistic conservatism. Again, the pronunciation /kən'trɒvəsɪ/ is now heard in official places, whereas the only accepted form was once /ˈkɒntrəvɜ·sɪ/.

Changes in usage and in the placing of word-stress are more notice-able than the more intimate phonemic changes and changes in intona-tion-patterns. And yet millions of television-viewers must be dimly aware that the ' speech-tunes ' of news-reel commentators in the nineteen-thirties (which they can hear regularly in programmes of a reminiscent nature) are very different from what we are used to to-day. Theatre-goers may notice that an acceptable ' a ' in ' man ', ' mad ', ' hat ', and so on is one much lower than the old statutory /æ/, and that young actors and actresses can now say something like /man/ or /mad/ or /hat/ (approaching the Lancashire /a/) without being rebuked. The vowel of ' mother ', ' butter ', ' shut ' has always been unstable. With many actors it seems to be moving from /ʌ/ and drawing close to /ɑ/.

But what no British speaker of English can fail to have noticed is the tendency of transatlantic English to assume a greater and greater hegemony. Those specifically American forms that were once smiled at in Edwardian drawing-rooms have now to be taken very seriously indeed. American English was once regarded as an amiable aberration from the East Midland norm, a ' colonial' dialect of English. Now we have to recognise that there is an American language—capable of immense variety within itself, but possessing enough general characteristics to be described summarily.

American English differs from British English of the BBC or ' standard' variety in certain important phonetic respects. It has resisted changes that British English accepted more than a century ago and, for the language of a progressive country, is remarkably conservative. Thus, it will not accept the so-called ' long A ' of ' bath ' (/bɑ:θ/) and clings to the Elizabethan front open vowel /æ:/, giving us /bæ:θ/. It insists on retaining a pronounced ' r ' in words like ' father ', ' darling ', ' park ', even though the sound is purely vestigial. It rejects the ' clear L ' and uses the ' dark ' variety in all positions, so that it opposes /ɫaɪk/ to British /laɪk/ (' like') and /ɫɪɫɪ/ to British /lɪɫi/ (' lily'). There are other differences, too, but these are the main ones, and, of all them, the opposition between /ɑ:/ and /æ:/ is the most considerable. The Standard British pronunciation of ' path ', ' dance ', ' can't' actively causes distress and even hostility in the United States, and British actors making films for export to America have to learn a kind of ' mid-Atlantic ' English whose main characteristic is that it meets the Americans on this question of the ' long A '.

American influence on pronunciation of English in the British territories is bound to be great, mainly because of the vast number of films, television programmes, and records of popular songs that fill our screens and record-players. For good or ill, the younger speakers of first-language English regard American pronunciation as a norm, and a teenager who wishes to disguise his regional or class accent finds it easier to do this by learning American rather than by attempting Standard English. At the same time, American educationists concerned with spreading English over the ' Free World ' naturally teach American phonemes, and these are enshrined in primers and records of a quality, and at a rate of distribution, that the British cannot touch. Some of the finest work on analysis of English, as well as on second-language teaching method, has been done in the University of Michigan. We need feel no surprise at the wholesale planting of American phonemes in foreign territories.

American speech attracts a British generation that is touchy about ' class ' and still hears in BBC English the voice of the squire with a whip or the sneering subaltern. There is about the best American English an informality, an ability to descend to solecisms like ' ain't ' or ' the mostest ' with no loss of dignity, that formal British English cannot match. On the other hand, American English—especially from the Pentagon—can be pompous with a pomposity that makes the hearer's heart sink like a plummet. Yet even the sesquipedalian ' affirmative ' for plain ' yes ' or such coinages as ' inhospitalisation ' seem to derive from a love of the sheer sound of language—a joy in the rumble of English cognate with the creative zest of American slang.

American locutions have been absorbed into British English ever since American English existed, though the rate of absorption has notably increased in the last thirty-five years—since, in fact, the coming of the talking films. Many American forms are, of course, native British English, usages which we abandoned long ago but which the conservative Americans have retained. ' Yeah ' for ' yes ' is as old as Anglo-Saxon ' gēa '; ' right now ' and ' I guess ' were common currency in the reign of Richard II. But other locutions point to immigrant Central European influence on American English, and many of them are too expressive to be regarded as the mere solecisms of the ignorant. ' This guy bugging you, honey ? ' is answered by ' He's offering me a film contract. You should bug me so good '. In this latter sentence we have a pure Yiddish construction, as also in the Rodgers-Hammerstein song : ' I'm a girl, and by me that's only great ' (the singer is a San Francisco Japanese). Even the consonant-group ' shm ' has come into American English from Yiddish ; its appearance in duplicated forms has brought new nuances to the language : ' Œdipus-shmoedipus,' said the Jewish lady to the psychiatrist ; ' what's it matter what he's got so long as he loves his mudder ? ' According to the American philological journal *Language*, the following was overheard in a university common-room : ' Your theory won't hold ; I've got data.'—' Data-shmata ; I *like* my theory.'

So much of the vigorous charm of American English derives from slang which, by its nature, must quickly die to make way for fresh slang. By the time ' That's the way the cookie crumbles ' has gone into British currency, it is already old hat in America. Beatnik terms (-*nik* is Jewish-Slavonic) and beatnik syntax (' Like he's crazy, man ') already have a lavender smell about them. The lure of the up-to-date is a sad one, but even flashy coinages keep language vigorous and remind us that it is a reflection of man's very mortal changeability.

There rests in American English, nevertheless, a sizeable body of usage which is there to stay and which points the American claim that its brand of language has a right to be regarded as distinct and different from British English. Such doublets as the following are well known (in each case the British word comes first) :

braces/suspenders	unbeautiful/homely
suspenders/garters	flat/apartment
lift/elevator	tap/faucet
pavement/sidewalk	underdone/rare
platform/track	undertaker/mortician
muffin/biscuit	stupid/dumb
biscuit/cracker	petrol/gas

There was a time when both Americans and Englishmen would be confused by these, and the many more, divergences. Now, thanks to British familiarity with American films, no Englishman feels these transatlantic usages to be really foreign. On the other hand, Americans continue to have difficulty with specifically British terms. This is because the propaganda traffic is one-way : eastwards.

England gladly buys American ; Americans have to be persuaded to reciprocate. It is interesting, and—for a patriot—disheartening, to see how many British-made television film series are designed with an American audience in view. British actors have to portray American characters, even when the locale is British ; or else American actors are imported to fill traditionally British rôles. There is one series in which Scotland Yard is virtually run by Americans, another in which a great hero of nineteenth-century Australia is an American carrier, yet another in which a Kenya police officer is Anglo-American (he derives his accent from his mother). In films like these, it is curious to hear odd Cockney supporting characters talking of seeing their attorneys, returning to their apartments, or waiting on the sidewalk. It is all a matter of buying and selling, commerce paving the way for the ultimate victory of American phonemes and American usage.

Ought we to lament this or attempt to halt it ? I think not. It is not really possible to resist such processes, however hard the forces of conservatism or inertia dump their dead weight on the threshold. English has a strange knack of doing well for itself, however much the old guard booms about threats to purity, the dangers of pollution. English did well out of the Danish and Norman invaders ; it will continue to profit from the strange loan-forms and coinages of the mixed populations that—in both England and America—represent the new ethnological order. Whatever form of English ultimately prevails— the British or the American variety—it will still be a great and rich and perpetually growing language, the most catholic medium of communication that the world has ever seen.

But, if we cannot really resist change, we can resist inflation, that debasement of language which is the saddest and most dangerous phenomenon of a world dominated by propaganda-machines, whether religious, political, or commercial. Propaganda always lies, because it over-states a case, and the lies tend more and more to reside in the words used, not in the total propositions made out of those words. A ' colossal ' film can only be bettered by a ' super-colossal ' one ; soon the hyperbolic forces ruin all meaning. If moderately tuneful pop-songs are described as ' fabulous ', what terms can be used to evaluate Beethoven's Ninth Symphony ? The impressionable young—on both sides of the Atlantic—are being corrupted by the salesmen ; they are being equipped with a battery of inflated words, being forced to evaluate alley-cat copulation in terms appropriate to the raptures of *Tristan and Isolde*. For the real defilers of language—the cynical inflators— a deep and dark hell is reserved.

Yet language survives everything—corruption, misuse, ignorance, ineptitude. Linking man to man in the dark, it brought man out of the dark. It is the human glory which antecedes all others. It merits not only our homage but our constant and intelligent study.

BIBLIOGRAPHY

I OWE a debt to all of the following. Some have given me ideas to agree or disagree with ; others have provided me with ready-made linguistic examples. All are recommended for further study.

BAUGH, A. C. *A History of the English Language* (London, 1954).
BLOOMFIELD, L. *Language* (New York, 1933).
BODMER, F. *The Loom of Language* (London, 1944).
FRIES, C. C. *The Structure of English* (New York, 1952).
JESPERSEN, O. *Growth and Structure of the English Language* (Leipzig, 1930).
JONES, D. *The Pronunciation of English* (Cambridge, 1956).
OGDEN, C. K. and I. A. RICHARDS. *The Meaning of Meaning* (London, 1946—8th edition).
QUIRK, R. *The Use of English* (London, 1962).
ULLMANN, S. *Semantics—an Introduction to the Science of Meaning* (Oxford, 1962).
WARD, I. C. *The Phonetics of English* (Cambridge, 1939—3rd edition).
WEEKLEY, E. *The Romance of Words* (London, 1917).
WYLD, H. C. *A History of Modern Colloquial English* (Oxford, 1936—3rd edition).

Primers

The ENGLISH UNIVERSITIES PRESS ' Teach Yourself ' Books :
Chinese—H. R. Williamson ; *Finnish*—A. H. Whitney ; *Hebrew*—R. K. Harrison ; *Malay*—M. B. Lewis ; *Modern Persian*—J. Mace ; *Russian*—M. Fourman ; *Welsh*—J. T. Bowen and T. J. Rhys Jones.

Dictionaries

English—The Shorter Oxford English Dictionary (1952).
French—Harrap's Standard French and English Dictionary, ed. J. E. Mansion (London, 1960).
Malay—An Abridged Malay-English Dictionary—R. J. Wilkinson, revised and enlarged A. E. Coope (London, 1948).
An English-Malay Dictionary—Sir Richard Winstedt (Singapore, 1952).
Russian—Collins' Russian-English English-Russian Dictionary—W. Schapiro (London, 1959).

APPENDIX ONE

The International Phonetic Alphabet—'Narrow' and 'Broad' Forms

THE form of the International Phonetic Alphabet used in this book is 'narrow': it has a separate symbol for every phoneme, and sometimes separate symbols for allophones. The reader may encounter a less exact version of this alphabet, especially in books which do not dig too deeply into the facts of speech ; this is the 'broad' form. It differs from the 'narrow' form only in the representation of vowel sounds, using lengtheners to show phonemic differences, thus :

/iː/—as in ' see ', ' sea ', ' me ', ' fee '
/i/—as in ' sit ', ' fish ', ' win ', ' dig '
/uː/—as in ' blue ', ' too ', ' few ', ' through '
/u/—as in ' put ', ' bull ', ' cook ', ' wool '
/ɔː/—as in ' saw ', ' for ', ' war ', ' daughter '
/ɔ/—as in ' got ', ' lock ', ' fog ', ' wad '
/əː/—as in ' fur ', ' her ', ' shirt ', ' word '

Sometimes, too, the reader may find that vowel sounds are doubled to indicate length, so that ' seat ' is shown as /siit/, ' moon ' as /muun/, and so on. Strictly speaking, we are at liberty to use whatever symbols we like, so long as we define them first.

APPENDIX TWO

How English Has Changed

VARIOUS translations of The Gospel According to St Matthew, Chapter 8, Verses 1 and 2.

(a) Anglo-Saxon, 995

(1) Sothlice tha se Haelend of tham munte nyther astah, tha fyligdon hym mycle maenio.

(2) Tha genealaehte an hreofla to him and hine to him geathmedde, and thus cwaeth, Drihten, gyf thu wylt, thu miht me geclaensian.

(b) Wyclif, 1389

(1) Forsothe when Jhesus hadde comen doun fro the hil, many cumpanyes folewiden hym.

(2) And loo ! a leprouse man cummynge worshipide hym, sayinge, Lord, yif thou wolt, thou maist make me clene.

(c) Tyndale, 1526

(1) When Jesus was come down from the mountayne, moch people folowed him.

(2) And lo ! there cam a lepre and worsheped him, saynge, Master, if thou wylt, thou canst make me clene.

(d) King James Version, 1611

(1) When he was come down from the mountain, great multitudes followed him.

(2) And, behold, there came a leper and worshipped him, saying, Lord, if thou wilt, thou canst make me clean.

(e) The New English Bible, 1961

After he had come down from the hill he was followed by a great crowd. And now a leper approached him, bowed low, and said, ' Sir, if only you will, you can cleanse me.'

INDEX